Chosen

A CALL THROUGH REFINEMENT TO PURPOSE

Published by Elite Foundation®, Fort Lauderdale, Florida
Book Cover: Jesus Cordero
Editorial Review: Elite Literary Team
Elite Foundation® is a registered trademark
Printed in the United States of America.

978-1-7360429-3-9 E-book
978-1-7360429-4-6 paperback

This publication is designed to provide accurate and authoritative information regarding the subject matter covered. It is sold with the understanding that the publisher is not engaged in rendering legal, accounting, clinical or other professional advice. If legal advice or other expert assistance is required, the services of a competent professional should be sought. The opinions expressed by the authors in this book are not endorsed by Elite Foundation and are the sole responsibility of the author rendering the opinion.

Most Elite Foundation® titles are available for bulk purchases for sales promotions, premiums, fundraising, and educational use. Special versions or book excerpts can also be created on direct request for specific needs aligned with Elite Foundation®

For more information , please write: Elite Foundation® Publisher
1451 West Cypress Creek Road, Suite 300, Ft. Lauderdale, Florida 33309
Or email: ElitePublisher@EliteFundsFreedom.org
Visit us online at: www.EliteFundsFreedom.org/book_program

Elite Foundation is a 501(c)(3) nonprofit organization that offers Indie publishing services to impact lives and community. When you Invest in Yourself, you Fund Freedom. Royalties from all our goods and services support scholarships/grants and the work done with victims and survivors of human exploitation and sex trafficking. Elite Foundation's vision is to eradicate the aftermath experienced by victims by creating a future for every survivor.

CHOSEN

A Call Through Refinement To Purpose

Elite Foundation® Publisher

Ft. Lauderdale, Florida

Inspired Stories of Real People with Unconquerable
Will to Thrive and Be Alive

CHOSEN

*"So, as those who have been chosen by God, holy and beloved,
put on a heart of compassion, kindness, humility, gentleness and
patience; bearing with one another, and forgiving each other,
whoever has a complaint against anyone; just as the Lord forgave
you, so also should you.*

*Beyond all these things put on love, which is the perfect
bond of unity.*

*Let the peace of Christ rule in your hearts, to which indeed
you were called in one body; and be thankful. Let the word of
Christ richly dwell within you, with all wisdom teaching and
admonishing one another with psalms and hymns and spiritual
songs, singing with thankfulness in your hearts to God. Whatever
you do in word or deed, do all in the name of the Lord Jesus, giving
thanks through Him to God the Father."*
~Colossians 3:12-17

i

Did you know that you are chosen?

Did you know that you are set apart?

Did you know that every strand of hair on your head and every cell in your body was preordained before you were conceived?

If your response to any of these questions is affirmation that you know that you are chosen then this read is uniquely for you. If in contrast you are unable to provide a response to any of these questions, then this read is especially for you. You see, no matter where you find yourself right now, this read will provide you with the insight that is applicable to your journey to actualizing exactly the character strengths and the outcome that you desire most in your life. You are probably thinking how can that be... how can this one text do all that?

Chosen was written in collaboration with people who share a heart to influence, impact, and to transform lives. It purports one message, that you are chosen, your Heavenly Father's masterpiece. Whether you are God fearing or not this read is relevant to you, by the simple fact that you exist on this planet at this time. There is no coincidence involved, only Truth. And in particular to womanhood, we have redefined the meaning. Our sisters did their part, by being courageous and breaking the silence. They spoke out, to give us a voice and platform to pursue meaning outside the stereotypical roles given to us and value in the world.

If you read through our historical lineage as women, it might not be readily evident but the truth is that we are God's masterpiece created in His image[1] and that He will complete the work through each of us, he started before His return[2]. Men and Women are God's light bearers in the world. However, too often this is a fleeting thought for women, as we become consumed by the details of our many roles and our requirements as daughters, sisters, mothers, wives, mentors, leaders etc.

We need to return to our original design, and to do so means to simply pursue to know your identity by who God says you are and to be obedient to the universal call of all Christians to evangelize the truth. Then your secondary callings based upon your passion(s) and purpose will become clear.

You are Chosen.

Not, by peers, teammates, or colleagues. Although it's always nice to be selected by people who are important in our life. To gain meaning through the eyes of others about oneself can at times actually be quite stifling to God's purpose for you.

The only caveat is that as human beings, our understanding at times has limits. When scientists of our generations examine our one central systemic organ that directs all else, our brains, it is realized that the mind is wired to default to negativity. This means that we must be intentional to change.

It is through the authors of Chosen that we provide alternate iterations of perception and perspective for you to consider, based on real life refining experiences that have culminated in the realization that each person has the choice to rise up to their Chosen call in obedience and reverence.

This read will equip you for growth and greater influence. It will require active engagement and there will be a tendency to assume that thoughts and beliefs that are part of your operating system, do not align with the wisdom shared on these pages. But this type of work, and it does take work, will ignite a level of actualization within you that will require that you leave parts of the old self behind, to transform into more of who you were created to be.

You are Chosen.

> *Now here we go. Come to the edge. We might fall. Come to the edge. It's too high! Come to the edge. And they came, and He pushed, and they flew.* - CHRISTOPHER LOG

Jessica Vera, Ph.D.
Award Winning Multiple Bestseller
Elite Foundation

HOW TO GET THE MOST FROM THE STORIES AND THE STUDY SECTIONS

This book is divided into three parts, each with a focused study section. In each part there is content of real stories of women who share transparently how God showed up in their worst moments in life, and how they learned that they were Chosen for such a time as this. The study section in each part of the book provides thematic content for personal and small group study.

PERSONAL & SMALL GROUP STUDY

Each of the books in the series of Inspired Stories of Real People with Unconquerable Will to Thrive and Be Alive that include Fearless, Invincible, Unstoppable, and Overcomer provide a different context of the experiences of transformation from the perspective of over 60 collaborative authors from the 21st century. Each story is unique, and adds to the social consciousness of humanity by providing insight into the mind, heart, and soul needs of people today, who are searching for their meaning and purpose in life.

Start by reading the short stories in this text and across the series. Then in the study section you will find content that will guide thought and promote discussion in a small group setting that leads to taking meaningful action. We were created to thrive in community, and we are called to elevate one another, as well as to rise up in unity for those still stifled by negative bonds. Rise up Chosen One!

A CALL TO THE SOURCE

Oftentimes, we want to gain but do not realize that in order to do so, it will certainly require refinement. In the world, popular culture teaches that relationships are transactional and therefore that there is something that is given in order to receive. In contrast, Truth teaches, those who believe in faith, that there is nothing that we can do to earn our redemption, freedom, salvation, as we are each imperfect. In fact, all was freely given through the sacrifice of our Creator, God. Sometimes these contradictions between the world view and the biblical view create ambivalence and disbelief, even dissonance within the body, primarily because we try to understand it from our perspective and don't realize that our perspectives are projections of our internal state in the moment. They are influenced by our senses and limited by our ability to conceptualize what is being experienced. For those, such as the writers who share their personal experiences of triumph over adversities in this text, the journey to refinement was laden with a lack of control, pain, and loss. Yet, the wisdom gained from some of the most heinous injustices perpetrated against women (the stealing of innocence, sexual identity, victimization, violence, and exploitation), resulted in the actualization of the very character traits that are found within those who are Chosen.

The Chosen share in the experience and strive to lead through compassion, kindness, humility, gentleness, and patience. There is a deep understanding of a need to serve others, to forgive self and others, and to be accepting of correction. Through a process of maturation we transform the old self into exactly who God ordained us to be. Not solely for the ego but for the other-centeredness that is actualized within when we manifest through the Holy Spirit.

CONTENT

PART I

CHOSEN FOR THE CHALLENGE

Purpose of the
Chosen Generation

by Antonece Johnson

It always sounds so cliché, when someone says the first step is always the hardest, but it is true. There is a tremendous amount of comfort that comes after taking the first step. I did not grow up living the American Dream. However, I knew there was happiness worthy of celebrating if I could take my first step towards it.

"For in it the righteousness of God is revealed from faith for faith, as it is written, "The righteous shall live by faith." (Romans 1:17).

My father's wallet was sitting on a table next to his ashtray. I could smell the scent of stale smoke lingering in the air just standing next to it. "Thou shall not steal." The words echoed in my head over and over, like a nagging little mosquito I wanted to swat. I stared at the wallet, feeling quite ambivalent. It was wrong, but I needed the money. I thought long and hard before deciding to open the wallet. It was empty. I did not know what to do. I sat in the recliner next to the wallet, feeling way more stressed than any young child should ever feel. Suddenly, I remembered that sometimes change would fall in the cracks of the chair. I stuck my small hand in the crevices. I pulled out a coin, and I smiled. It was a quarter. I stuck my hand in again and I pulled out a few more coins. I went to all the couches and found more coins: a quarter, two dimes, one nickel, and three pennies. I was so excited but afraid at the same time. "Yes, I'm going to grandma's house!"

That day, I committed to finding something more. After tucking the coins into my pocket, I went into the kitchen and took two bottles from the sink. I rinsed them with boiling water just like mom had shown me. Next, I filled each of the bottles with milk and shook them up. I put the cap on them and placed them in the baby's bag. Finally, I went into my baby brother Chris's room, which he shared with my older brother, who was only nine. I grabbed a diaper and a change of clothes and placed them in the baby's bag. Chris was lying quietly in the crib. With one finger, I checked to see if he was wet and changed him, then I swaddled him in his blanket, I placed the packed bag over my shoulders. I waved goodbye to my little sister Teresa, who was only five, and my brother Jr. who was only ten months older than I was.

When I opened the door, I closed my eyes for a moment, took a deep breath, and walked out. Walking through the neighborhood alone, I searched for a route that seemed familiar to me. A few blocks into my journey, I found the city bus stop not too far from my house. Finally, the bus arrived. I held my baby brother as tightly as I could with his bag on my shoulder and climbed up the step to enter the bus. The driver was a middle-aged Black man with an afro. "Where are you going, young lady?" he asked. "I want to go to my Grandma's house in Hollywood." I dropped all the coins in his hands and walked to an open seat.

The bus finally started moving. I silently celebrated in my head at the thought of seeing my grandmother. Moments later, the bus stops, and the door opens. The bus driver is motioning to the passenger to look in my direction. To my surprise, it was my mother gliding down the aisle towards me. My heartbeat was so fast that I felt it at the bottom of my feet. She looked at me, but I could not tell by her glance what she was thinking. The look on her face was different than when she was angry. She took Chris from my arms and motioned for me to get up. We stepped off the bus and made our way towards the house. She was quiet and very calm for almost the entire walk home. "Why did you leave?" she asked, waiting for my response. "Daddy beats you, and you let him." My mother was again silent. "Am I going to get a spanking?" "No, but you have to tell your dad why you ran away," she said. That night I laid in my bed waiting for my spanking, but it did not happen.

This memory from my childhood reminds me of the blind faith I had as a child. My only fear was taking the first step out of my front door. Since I was often told "No", I was inexperienced with making a choice that was not my own. To my benefit, I was too young to think about consequences, or what someone would think of me, or any of the excuses we used to talk our adult selves out of when making tough choices. I only knew that I had reached my threshold of unhappiness and was no longer willing to sit in someone else's choice or someone else's comfort zone. I had to learn to exercise on my own. We stay in spaces physically and mentally where we are not happy to be, because we lack the courage to make necessary choices. We force ourselves to live in someone else's comfort zone and eventually make it our own, even when painful. After making the first step out the door of my home, I experienced what it felt like to be courageous. The strength that came along with exercising my right to choose required me to push past any fear or doubt and act. That requires faith.

"For as the body without the spirit is dead, so faith without works is dead also." (James 2:26).

Approximately, three years had passed, and I was eleven years old. I heard a high-pitched scream coming from my parents' room. I looked at my little sister, who was about 8 years old. We knew all too well what that sound meant. Rishit! That is what we called my father, named Richard, when he could not hear us. I looked at my coloring book, hoping I could tune out the noises, but I could not. Suddenly, my mother ran out of the room and my father swiftly followed behind her. My siblings and I peeked our heads outside of our rooms and saw my father pick up a hammer and swing it at my mother, narrowly missing her. My mother ran back into the room, and my father dropped the hammer on the dining table and ran behind her. I turned to my siblings, and said, "We have to tell someone!" Once again, I faced having to take the first step out my door alone.

Even though it was very dark outside, this time was easier because it was familiar to me. There was no fear of being caught, only a commitment to get to my destination. With bare feet, I ran to my neighbor next door, who was an older Caribbean couple, and explained what happened. The wife asked her husband to check it out while she called the cops. I made my way back into my house before the neighbor knocked. My father answered and said that my mother was sleeping and could not come to the door. When the man left, my father came to my room, where my three siblings were with me. He asked who left the house. Everyone denied leaving, and I remained quiet.

That night my mother found her courage and ran out the door to that same neighbor. The cops came shortly after, and we left my father for the last time. We made it to Grandma's house safely. Before that incident, my father would apologize, and we would go back. Together, we committed to never go back.

There is rarely a worse feeling than a child hearing the screams from their mother at the hands of their father. My mother knew this feeling all too well since she experienced my grandmother being abused when she was a child. My mother committed to holding on to a relationship far too long to keep the family together, even though it almost killed her. I imagine my grandmother did the same. I vowed to break that cycle of abuse and never allow myself to be in that situation.

When I was 15, I met Tim. He told me he was 19, but I later found out he was much older. That vast age difference allowed him to manipulate and control me without knowing. A couple of years into the relationship, I had moved out of my mother's home and into a small rundown apartment. I went to school and worked two jobs. Eventually, Tim moved to Georgia and convinced me to move in with his mother until I finished my first two years at the community college. Then, I would follow him to Clark University. After moving in with his mother, Tim grew more controlling, and with the distance between us, he was constantly belittling and yelled when he thought his control over me slipped. Whenever I would break off the relationship, he would apologize and beg me to stay.

He started pressuring me to have a child. I was 21, and I had just started my career as a technical support consultant and did well for myself. Growing up in a conservatively strict Christian home, my mom taught me to wait for marriage before having sex or having kids. I told him I did not want to have a child because we were not married, and we were both still in school. He told me he would give me a promise ring and his mother would help me take care of the baby. It appalled me.

After 5 years of being in the relationship, I finally realized I didn't even want to be in it anymore. Somehow, I felt stuck in these decisions that I allowed him to make for me and adopted them as my own. I trained myself to make sure he was comfortable while avoiding the fact that I was uncomfortable with the verbal abuse, cheating, and added pressure to be a single mother. I replaced the blind faith I had as a child with doubt, shame, and fear. I held myself responsible for giving him a part of me he did not deserve for years. I remembered the commitment I made when I was a child to break the cycle of abuse. Yet, like my grandmother and my mother, I was unhappy and stuck in the same situation. I unknowingly made daily commitments to punish myself. Guilt and conviction kept me in a relationship that nearly cost me my life.

Finally, I decided it was time to celebrate my new career and all the good things happening in my life, but I could not do that without taking purposeful action. I had to make new commitments which involved me introspectively looking at all the moments I never celebrated because I was afraid to take the first step out the door like I did when I was 8. First, I had to forgive myself, and that required grace. Looking for apartments and new furniture for my own space gave me a glimpse of what happiness looked like for me. I realized that my dreams of independence were not as far-fetched as I made them out to be. All I needed to do was choose to leave.

After the usual begging, followed by tears that did not work, Tim made three attempts to kill me within two months. He was arrested and served about 3 years for attacking me before they released him. I lived in constant fear, because the last time I spoke with him, he vowed to finish what he started when he was released. Sadly, he met a 23-year-old young mother, who he dated for about six months before he murdered her. After being on the run for 2 days, he turned himself in and is now serving a life sentence. God saved my life!

"He saved us, not because of works done by us in righteousness, but according to his own mercy, by the washing of regeneration and renewal of the Holy Spirit" (Titus 3:5 ESV).

Many years had passed. I moved on with my life. I was happy and comfortable, but something was always missing. Although I was a wife and a mother to an amazing son, had a magnificent job, living in a beautiful home in a pleasant neighborhood, I did not feel fulfilled. I struggled many years with what I now know as "Survivor's Remorse." When Tim murdered that young woman, who had children aged 2, and 3, I felt a sense of guilt. My life was saved, hers was not. I did not know how he could have made three attempts and not be successful. He drove me off the road and totaled my car. He knocked me out and tried to stab me with a knife, and then there was the third attempt when he drove to my job with a gun. Each time, someone intervened to protect me. Secretly, I carried a tremendous weight, not understanding why God preserved my life. Certainly, I wanted to live, I just did not know why I was living. I was not fulfilling my purpose, and I felt like I was letting God down.

It took 15 years of sitting in my comfort zone of what appeared to be the American Dream, before realizing that there, I would never find my purpose. Finding my purpose would require me to move beyond the walls of my home and get involved in the community. I discovered that our purpose in life is not about self, but the lives we touch, bless, and improve daily.

I started writing for film and produced a documentary on what I learned about preventing and creating awareness against Sex Trafficking. The documentary allowed me to give victims of trauma a voice. The weight of "Survivor's Remorse" lifted from my shoulders. I often tell people that when you walk in your purpose, you will know. The feeling is hard to describe. Today I know who I am. I am the 4th generation curse breaker! The history of domestic violence and trauma ends with me. Throughout my life, the 7 components that guide me to survive trauma also empowers me to walk in my purpose are commitment, comfort, clarity, choice, challenge, courage, and the ability to celebrate.

Trauma, grief, and suffering are inevitable. Coupled with feelings of fear, sadness, and pain, we find ourselves stuck in relationships far too long to keep the family together, to avoid the stigma of divorce or the humiliation of having to explain why we left or stayed so long. We feed ourselves poisonous excuses which become daily affirmations that lead us to become unfulfilled and unhappy. They hold us hostage in generational curses because we suffer in silence. That silence is the fuel the enemy needs to thrive on for generations to come. You are not alone.

"The Lord is long-suffering, and of great mercy, forgiving iniquity and transgression, and by no means clearing the guilty, visiting the iniquity of the fathers upon the sons to the third and fourth generation" (Numbers 14:18 KJV).

Before anyone else, commit to 'your' happiness. When you feel unfulfilled, evaluate the comfort zone you are sitting in and make sure it is your own. You will never find your purpose when you are comfortable, or surely not in someone else's comfort zone. When you feel stuck, it means that you lack clarity around what you want. Refocus. Then, write the choices you need to make and take small steps towards them. Adversity may arise but challenge yourself to push past your fears. Do not allow them to hold you back. You will experience the beauty of courage after you have taken the first step. Remember that choice is a muscle that when exercised, its weight becomes easier, and you become stronger.

Last, but not least, celebrate. Celebrating is not about winning; it is about acknowledging the action of taking the first step and the lessons learned on your journey. You will never celebrate if you do not start. When you start, you gain the experience to win. You deserve to be happy.

Generational curses are the devil's food. It is the nutrition he counts on. He eats for free, while starving generation after generation and sucking the life from countless families. As a result, we become deficient in happiness, love, or anything that allows us to thrive. When the generational curses in my family were broken, I experienced true joy and a peace that surpasses understanding. The clarity I have now is this, Tim, the young woman who he tragically murdered, both of my grandmothers, grandfathers, my mother, and my father all paid a high price for my freedom. They were all victims due to the sins of their fathers'. There were many weapons formed against me throughout my life, but they did not prosper because I am the 4th generation. From my mother's womb God chose me to fulfill every purpose he planned for my life. I only needed to follow the path He laid out for me.

"Trust in the Lord with all your heart and lean not on your own understanding; In all your ways acknowledge Him, And He shall direct your paths" (Proverbs 3:5-6, NKJV).

Today, my head has been lifted, and I am fulfilled. I can truly appreciate my journey. I rejoice in knowing that my son, the royal priesthood, will grow up in a healthy home. As a filmmaker, working with amazing people and lending a creative vision to their stories to help save lives, fuels my God-given purpose. I celebrate the relationships and mentorships I have maintained that help

10

me grow daily. I am forever thankful for God's continual shield of protection over me. Becoming a best-selling author, knowing all the lives this book will impact gives honor to God providing a path to healing and restoration for future generations.

"But you, O Lord, are a shield about me, my glory, and the lifter of my head." (Psalm 3:3 ESV).

"But you are a chosen generation, a royal priesthood, a holy nation, His own special people, that you may proclaim the praises of Him who called you out of darkness into His marvelous light" (1 Peter 2:9, NKJV).

Antonece Johnson, warmly called Neicey, by her friends and family, is a Product Manager for a tech company, and a South Florida native. While giving survivors a voice in her Director's debut documentary series Taking Innocence Project, Neicey has also embraced her role as an advocate raising awareness against Sex Trafficking, which is the subject of the series. On the Executive Advisory Board Member for Elite Foundation, Mrs. Johnson serves as the Chair for the Information Technology Committee. She also serves as an Executive Advisor to politicians focusing on strategy and business development working on community projects to create peace in a world where a Pandemic and Civil unrest have served up chaos.

In her chapter, Neicey shares stories about her history of trauma while inspiring others that have found themselves stuck in generational curses to take their rightful place as the Chosen 4th generation to break them.

Neicey can be found on social media

https://www.facebook.com/neicey.johnson1/ and
https://www.instagram.com/neiceycurl/
Follow the Documentary Taking Innocence Project
https://www.facebook.com/TakingInnocence/

The Chosen Road

by Sandra Maria Anderson

"I chose you before I formed you in the womb; I set you apart before you were born. I appointed you a prophet to the nations" (Jeremiah 1:5)

"Are we there yet?" My children would say as we made our way Northbound on Interstate 95. I still smile when memories of the road move past my mind: The clouds above us; my children in the backseat singing along to Neil Diamond's song 'Forever in Blue Jeans.' The bumps on the road from unexpected potholes and debris remind me that the ache is gone now. Only the lessons linger on in my memory. Lessons that time, alone, could not teach. Thus, understanding is key.

After some time in the backseat, my children's impatience would get the best of them. "Mom, are we there yet?" They would moan before singing along with the next song on the radio. "Be patient. We will get there soon." I'd say with a smile, peering in the backseat through the rearview mirror. Whether Walt Disney World in Orlando, a trip we took one Summer to New York, and all the adventures in between, I understand how long the journey can seem. I know all too well that it's human nature to want to be in control, to see where the road leads, and how long it will take to get there. Today, as a mother and a grandmother, I feel so blessed to teach the next generations the most valuable lessons I have learned on my journey. Lessons on the illusion of control, lessons on truth and love. Lessons on the importance of having a sense of purpose and on divine roadblocks. Although the road seemed so long, I am grateful that God preserved my life for such a time as this. I understand why often God chooses the broken road to get us to trust the Chief Navigator finally. The Old Testament writings teach us that broken roads are a part of our faith journey while on the chosen road:

"Many are the afflictions of the righteous, but the LORD delivers him out of them all" (Psalm 34:19, NKJV).

Nothing made sense during the early years. How could a loving God allow such pain and chaos? I felt my world was broken, lost, and irreparably damaged. The depression and anxiety of not knowing what was next in my life were almost worse than the reasons why.

When I was a child, I tried to make meaning of a road I couldn't fully understand. The way the tires would roll into the bumps and the potholes, jolting me around in the back seat like a directionless ragdoll when the social workers drove me to the next shelter or foster home. I lost count of the shelter homes, foster families, and moments I'd spend counting the days before I was on the road again, off to someplace new. It didn't take long for me to realize that unpacking was a waste of time. "Not a good fit," the caseworker mumbled beneath her breath, glancing at a hand full of files before we drove away to the next place of rejection and disappointment. "Whatever." I'd whisper, trying to mask the sadness with sarcasm, sick and tired of case managers, backseats, moving around from place to place, and being me.

After some time, I begin to refer to each new place as my Neverland. It seemed no matter where I landed, I could never quite fit in, and much like the lost boys in Peter Pan, I thought this was my lot, my fate. I felt cursed by some dark shadow to live this way. Secret pain has a way of growing like sharp thorns on a rose bush. Thorns that over time became a defense to keep others out and a cage that kept me locked away inside the shame and despair of the crimes against my life; this was the birth of self-pity. Like a slow poison to the soul, self-pity, over time, breeds self-destruction.

How do we make sense of what we have no language to understand or explain? I was only 12 years old back then, but the road still reminds me again and again that I am not my own. I just didn't know it at the time. Before that point, I developed the habit of twirling the edge of my blouse around my finger until it became so painful that the rest of me would go numb. Numb to the clamoring noise in my head that still echoes even though I'm miles away from a house I once called home. Numb to the secrets of 24th street and the monsters that came in-between. And numb to every other desire except the need to be left alone. For a long time, I had a real fear of everything and everyone. Trauma can do that to you.

In the beginning, I had dreams of joining the military, serving my country with courage and pride. Yes, I knew at a young age exactly what I wanted to do when I grew up. My Justice League comic books reinforced that dream within me. The Army was my branch of choice. I figured after serving for about ten years, I would join the police force and then retire in a quiet community.

I could have never imagined the course of events that would send my world in a complete tailspin. It started with my parents' divorce. I had no language to express how it broke my heart and made the world feel lonely and unsure. The aftermath of addiction, rage, and infidelity impacts the entire family, especially the most vulnerable: the children.

Seen and not heard, I learned to obey the unspoken rules that mandate "what goes on in this house, stays in this house." During that time, the numbness was better than the feelings of fear—the dread of not knowing where the road would lead to next. So, tighter and tighter, I'd twirl my finger inside my blouse until the pressure turned to pain, and the pain morphed into the sweet void of numbness. Strange how the pain from twisting my finger in my blouse gave me a sense of power and control in a world that seemed utterly out of control.

My mother remarried, and then the sexual abuse began, and like an angry storm, it blew all my dreams away. Terrible things happen behind closed doors. I was seven years old. My childhood had vanished with the whack of my stepfather's hand and two magazines; one was full of bullets, the other, with pornography. Fierce storms continued. At age 11, I ran away from home to find my father, but the cruel arms of human traffickers found me instead. After being sold to a man named Edward on Fort Lauderdale beach, I told myself that I would not live to see 20. By the time the Broward County police incidentally rescued me, rage and shame had already become my new pimps. The Department of Children and Families did their best to provide food, clothes, and shelter for my broken life. But something was missing because what they offered did not keep the memories of the monster's touch away. History was about to play its encore of generational trauma.

The Apostle Paul's message provides the solution to the formidable issue of recidivism in rehabs, prisons, and every other social service institution known to man:

"And He said to me, "My grace is sufficient for you, for My strength is made perfect in weakness." Therefore, most gladly I will rather boast in my infirmities, that the power of Christ may rest upon me" (2 Corinthians 12:9, NKJV).

What we don't know will hurt not only us but also future generations. Full speed ahead, the unresolved grief and trauma led to further victimization. I lived in a constant state of fight or flight. I became a master of running away from every perceived threat, disguising the deep pain and the relentless shame that accused me of being too weak to fight back. Still, the storms continued. Pregnant at 13, hospitalize suicide attempt at 15, crack cocaine addiction at 16, a convicted felon at 18, and in the early 1990s, an AIDS diagnosis. By all appearances, my life was irreparable. I didn't know that amidst all the chaos and tragedy of my shattered life were seeds planted in the fertile soil of my childhood, growing roots among the weeds of adversity. Powerful seeds of determination, strength, and resilience began to surface, breaking through the cracks of all the trauma and heartache.

In my family, Joyce, my eldest sister, taught us stories of God from a very young age. I remember the storms in Tampa. As we sat atop of the stairs, it was Joyce teaching us of the mysteries of God, the miracles of His hands, and the faithfulness of His love that anchored my young soul. She would sing sweet lullabies over us at night, especially the scary nights when the fights between our parent's civil war grew louder than the storms outside. Today, I can still hear her say, "No matter what, you must trust in God. I never told Joyce of my dreams to join the military and become a law enforcement officer. I never got the chance after my parents' divorce. Yet somehow, Joyce prepared me for the most formidable military: God's Army. Mature beyond her years, she cared for us, cooking, cleaning, checking our homework, and teaching us the faithful love of the one true living God.

My basic training began with her devotion, bible stories, and tender discipline. She taught us that God does not always save us from adversity, but He is faithful to bring us through every trial and storm. Those early years shaped my character like nothing else could. Her voice still echoes across time, especially now. Joyce is with the Lord, and how my heart ever misses her loving voice and soothing lullabies.

In the Spring of 2004, Christ, the Chief Navigator, led me to the place where my life would drastically change. I was desperate, wanting to break free from the tyranny of domestic violence, shame, and a lifetime of secret thorns. I still had a long way to go to achieve a sense of wellness and self-mastery. I was ready for the road that would lead me to find my voice, confidence, and inner strength. It was now or never. I stood at the base of the mountain known as Pikes Peak in Colorado Springs, Colorado. I believe faith can move mountains, but still, there are others we must climb. Without a doubt, I knew I had to climb to find the voice of a little girl that was calling out to me. There, one step at a time, I begin to climb out of what felt like a lifelong trench: a deep gorge of childhood trauma, violence, and sexual exploitation. As I reached 10,000 feet, I could barely breathe. I felt the demons of rage, shame, and despair, losing air, gasping, falling back, unable to reach me at this high altitude where God was leading me. After two days of hiking, I stepped on the summit of Pikes Peak. The journey out of the trenches led me to an elevation of 14,115 feet. It was a glorious experience.

There, amidst silvery clouds and rock cliffs as big as the eyes can see, I fell to my knees in gratitude for all God has carried me through. He has been faithful. I remember in those moments the voice of a little girl that I once knew. She stood there in my memory, flawless and beautiful. Her carefree smile let me know that everything would be alright, despite all that had happened in my life and all the challenges ahead. Somehow, I heard her voice, and the Chief Navigator led me to find the soul of the little girl I once was, healed and whole. He was there all the time. God never left her alone. He is the restorer of every lost soul (Psalms 23:3). There are times we will feel forsaken, forgotten, and lonely. The truth is we are never alone.

"Be strong and of good courage, do not fear nor be afraid of them; for the LORD your God, He is the One who goes with you. He will not leave you nor forsake you" (Deuteronomy 31:6, NKJV).

The Chief Navigator is careful to lead us. Yet, without adversity, we cannot practice the fruit of the spirit of love for our enemies, joy in sadness, peace in uncertainty, longsuffering in hardship, gentleness in a hostile situation, goodness in a world of sin, and faith amid storms. In adversity, we have the excellent opportunity to practice Christlike character, thus proving we are His disciples. For many years, I would cause my own suffering because of unresolved grief and trauma, not understanding that we perish because we lack knowledge (Hosea 4:6). What we don't understand creates encores of revictimization and trauma.

"Get wisdom! Get understanding! Do not forget, nor turn away from the words of my mouth. Do not forsake her, and she will preserve you; Love her, and she will keep you. Wisdom is the principal thing; Therefore, get wisdom. And in all your getting, get understanding" (Proverbs 4:5-7, NKJV).

For that reason, the healing process requires us to be teachable. I needed information to help me understand how to make sense of what I had no language to explain. I had to gain self-awareness. Below the surface, subconscious drivers were leading me to self-destruct from the inside out. I had to obtain the right attitude and recognize how trauma subconsciously influenced my thoughts and behaviors. I had to mature beyond my cynicism to trust and understand God's faithfulness to help me through the journey of wholeness. Soon, I began the excavation process, the purposeful act of digging through the past, unearthing the skeletons of repressed memories. I didn't want to feel again, but as they began to take on the skin, I had to move beyond the numbness. I had to allow myself to process the memories, to cry, and to heal. Ultimately, I learned to self-regulate and gained the personal liberty to choose my actions beyond my survival mode reactions. Letting go of all the pain, rage, and self-pity freed me from my traumatic past. I became free to see the reality of God's amazing love for all of humanity, including my traffickers and all those who cause my deepest pain. In Christ, we are free to love our enemies and to forgive them wholeheartedly.

"Therefore, if the Son makes you free, you shall be free indeed" (John 8:36, NKJV).

From the beginning, God's plan for our life is eternal peace and salvation through faith in Christ. I realized that God, the Chief Navigator, was there all the time. My journey of overcoming complex trauma to experiencing the unspeakable joy and peace just might be your story, too.

The Spirit of God does not reside in the noise and clamor of our fears and anxieties. Nor does He move through the human striving of piety, church attendance, self-righteousness, or legalism. God's Gifts are not for sale, nor will religious conjuring of mysticism mock His glory. Salvation is the gift of God, offered to us by grace through faith in Christ alone, and not of ourselves:

"For by grace you are saved through faith, and that not of yourselves; it is the gift of God, not of works, lest anyone should boast" (Ephesians 2:8-9, NKJV).

Life is busy with highways and side streets that we must traverse every day. Where the road leads us is determined by our choices rather than our circumstances. Perception is everything, and healing from unresolved grief and trauma will subsequently heal our flawed perception. The choice is ours, to turn right or left; to stop on the tracks of indecision or press the gas of impulsivity. We must choose to allow God to order each turn by the gentle whispers of the Holy Spirit. Life is all about choices! I've taken many roads in life, but only one has led me to peace, purpose, and truth.

The broken road showed me that we desperately need a Savior. The original sin in the Garden of Eden and the sequence of traumatic events since that time distorts our perception of truth. In the book of Luke 23:34, Jesus said, "Father, forgive them, for they do not know what they are doing." Toward the end of Christ's life, just below His nailed pierced feet, they divided up his clothes by casting lots, not knowing who they were crucifying, nor did they know that they could not take His life. Still, for the sake of love, Christ gave His life for the sins of the world.

When I look around the world today, I see the broken road that has led many astray in their search for hope, for life, liberty, and the pursuit of happiness. Corrupt leaders in government, churches, and families expose a more profound truth of the brokenness of humankind and the need for redemption. Yet, there is nothing new under the sun (Ecclesiastes 1:9). From the days of King Saul, the first king of Israel, to Germany's Adolph Hitler, evidence shows that we are desperately lost without the Spirit of God ruling our lives.

Yet, century after century, community leaders and lawmakers continue to grapple with the problem of sex trafficking, child abuse, corruption, poverty, and on and on. Above all systems of the world, God's kingdom alone will reign. Above new age beliefs, secular worldviews, and spiritualism, His Holy Spirit is the only moral compass for humanity's survival. Our faith and trust in His Holy word prove we are His own:

"But without faith, it is impossible to please Him, for he who comes to God must believe that He is and that He is a rewarder of those who diligently seek Him" (Hebrews 11:6, NKJV).

Faith is the way of the Chosen Road. And in 1 Peter 4:12, the disciple Christ referred to as the "Rock" informs us that we should not think that it is strange when we go through "fiery trials," as though we are cursed or the victim of misfortune. On the contrary, God knows exactly where we are and where the road is leading.

"Beloved, do not be surprised at the fiery trial when it comes upon you to test you, as though something strange was happening to you…" (1 Peter 4:12, ESV).

The Chosen road comes with a great promise from God: the divine turn that offers us an eternal perspective through the eyes of faith in Christ to declare:

"that we were "bought at a price; therefore, we glorify God in body and in spirit, which is God's" (1 Corinthians 6:20, NKJV).

I am a part of the chosen generation of believers; the ancestral curse breakers sent to set the captives free and to declare the kingdom of God is here! The Chosen road reminds me that I share in the suffering of Christ; therefore, I rejoice in afflictions. Christ's glory is revealed in us through the Spirit of God when we are patient in adversity. When I look back on the road that I've traveled and witness how God protected and preserved my life, my heart sings of His loving-kindness! He is faithful unto a thousand generations. He is the Chief Navigator. His timing is impeccable, His love is unfailing, and His grace is sufficient no matter what the future holds.

We will get there!

We can be confident that "He that sits upon the throne makes all things new. For He has said, for these words are true and faithful. I am Alpha and Omega, the Beginning and the end. I will give unto him that is a thirst of the fountain of the water of life freely. He that overcomes shall inherit all things, and I will be his God, and they shall be my people" (Rev. 21:5-7). His grace will navigate us all the way home. His promise still stands. Great is His faithfulness

Sandra Maria Anderson is the founder of Love Gardens Ministries International, Inc., a nonprofit, holistic mentorship, and counseling program that teaches, empowers, and transforms the lives of individuals, families, and communities. Sandra is a mother, grandmother, doctoral student, and advocate of health and wellness. She is also a speaker, fitness instructor, and the author of Lessons from the Thorns, an autobiography that chronicles her fight for mental health and wellness.

Through her faith, Sandra has overcome insurmountable odds, including childhood sexual abuse at the age of seven and sex trafficking at 11 years old. Her tumultuous life led to her placement in the Department of Children and Families (DCF) at 12 years old. She became pregnant at 13 years old and continued in DCF custody, foster, and shelter homes. Her life presented her with a front-row seat, witnessing domestic violence to survive it. The trauma led her to crack cocaine addiction at 16 and a 1987 drug-sting arrest captured on national TV by the Broward County Sheriff's Office during the "War on Drugs." We all have a story.

In 1990, faith in God and her fight for education freed Sandra from drug and alcohol addiction. In 1994, she was awarded Alumni of the year in nursing from the BETA program by Commissioner Clay Shaw. In 2009, Sandra earned her bachelor's degree in Human Services, and later, in 2013, she received her Master's in Leadership at Palm Beach Atlantic University. Today, Sandra attends Liberty University as a doctoral student studying Community Care and Counseling Marriage and Family Therapy.

As Founder of Love Gardens Ministries, Sandra hopes to halt the transmission of trauma in families by increasing awareness of why we do what we do and getting to the problem's source.

To contact Sandra, please go to:

Website: sandramariaanderson.com
Facebook: Sandra Maria Anderson
Email: drsandramarialgmi@gmail.com
Phone: 561-584-2051

Put It on Pause

by Gail Moore

I am a 'PK', all my life I was raised in the church. If you are unfamiliar with the term PK, it is short for pastor's kid. With six brothers" and sisters' life had its ups and downs. We lived in the inter-city and I went to church 7 days a week non stop. I would always say to myself "when I get grown, I am never going to church again" LOL! I went to church so much I thought my middle name was church ha-ha! So, one Sunday I decided to fake like I was sick, hoping my mom would let me stay home. I started coughing and clearing my throat, sniffling, using a fake sick voice. I said; "Momma, I don't feel good, can I stay home today." She prayed in the name of Jesus you are healed, now let's go to church. So, as you can see, staying home from church was not an option. We were not allowed to listen to secular music, go to parties or use profanity in our house. If you did, you would get blacky. Now, you are probably wondering what is blacky? Blacky was the belt my father wore around his waist, so whenever you chose to break rules, you would get blacky. So, I grew up listening to Mahalia Jackson, Shirley Caesar, and James Cleveland. I loved music. At the age of seven my mother recognized I had the ability to play piano by ear. So, she made me practice every day after school, eventually, practicing piano became my favorite thing to do. Going to school in the inter-city exposed me to a lot of different kinds of people. We called them, unchurched people, and this is my story.

We met in high school my sophomore year. I remember walking to school and seeing him standing there smoking a cigarette looking so handsome. He would smile, wave and my heart would skip a beat. He was my Boo! I had a crush on him, and he had an even bigger one on me. Although I knew he was a drug dealer and a compulsive gambler, that did not matter, I was in love, and we walked to school together every day. We continued seeing each other even though he was always in and out of jail, I would wait until he got out and we continued seeing each other like nothing ever happened. If my parents found out I was seeing a drug dealer, I knew I would get blacky, so I chose to make him my high school sweetheart secret. We ate lunch in the cafeteria together and saw each other between classes. Soon those morning walks to school became morning walks to the park and skipping school. In no time, I was smoking marijuana, drinking alcohol, and using cocaine on a regular basis. School became unimportant to me, and my grades dropped miserably.

One night, a neighbor called my mom to ask if I could babysit her 3-month-old for a few hours. I knew my mother would say no, because we had to be at church, surprisingly she said yes, I was shocked and happy I did not have to go to church. While mom dressed for church, the phone rang, "It was him" Fear shot through my body like a bolt of lightning. He told me there was a party at the YMCA tonight and he wanted me to come. For fear of blacky, I quickly said ok and rushed him off the phone. Later I walked across the street to babysit. They welcomed me in, and the baby was in his crib playing with a little rattle, he was adorable! They told me to help myself to whatever I wanted in the fridge, handed me the baby's bottle and off they went. I played with him for a while, fed him his bottle, rocked him to sleep and placed him back in his crib. He was fast asleep. There I was, sitting and watching tv, but all I could think about was going to the party to meet my boyfriend.

The YMCA was just down the street so I decided while the baby was asleep, I would go to the party, and get back before anyone knew. Yep, you guessed it right, I left the baby in his crib unattended, and I went to the party. We were dancing and drinking like there was no tomorrow and I forgot all about the time. While drinking and laughing with friends, I felt a tap on my shoulder. I turned to see who it was, and to my surprise! it was my cousin. He told me my mother called his mother looking for me and that I was in big trouble. I panicked and he drove me home immediately. I didn't even say goodbye to my boyfriend.

I knew I was in big trouble with blacky. I got back home, and quietly opened the back door. I could hear voices coming from the living room. I walked into the living room and there stood two police officers, the parents of the infant I was supposed to have been babysitting, and my mother and father. I could tell my parents were furious, and they had every right to be. Any time you chose to ride with Satan he will always take you further then you want to go. The next thing I remember, was seeing blacky sliding threw daddy's belt loops. I got the beating of my life. Back then it was called discipline, today it is called child abuse.

A year had passed, I was a Junior in high school, and he was in jail again, this time for a while. One day my best friend, Paula

Fuller wanted to try out for the band. She insisted we try out together. So, I agreed, we tried out and made it! I was now a high stepper and a member of the San Diego High School Band. We would march, twirling our batons every Friday night for the football games with hundreds of people in the stands. I loved the excitement of it all.

Our band director was very stern, we had to be at band practice every day and being late was unacceptable. But, in order to get to the band hall, I had to go through the piano room where piano classes were held. I had never seen that room before. There were pianos all over the room. I felt like a kid in a candy store. So, I sat down to play for a few minutes and rushed off to band practice. Every day on my way to band practice I would sit down to play the piano only meaning to be there for a few minutes, but I loved playing and singing so much, each time I would play longer and longer causing me to be late for band practice, and eventually I was permanently dismissed from the band. But I did not mind.

I continued going to the piano room to practice piano on my lunch break, until, one day I got word my boyfriend was out of jail and he was looking for me. It had been a while, but I was still happy to see him. One day after school we stopped by his house. While we were there, he asked if I would do him a favor? He handed me a brown package with tape wrapped tightly all around it. I noticed it had no name or address on it. He told me he wanted me to make a drop for him, promised I would be safe, and the pay would be worth it. I knew he was asking me to transport drugs for him. But I did not want that kind of life. I want to do more than skip school, drugs and end up in jail like him. So, I broke up with him for good.

They always say, if you want to know where you are going in life just look at the people you are hanging out with. Oftentimes people you meet do not really know who you are, and they cannot always see your worth. That is why it is important for you to know who you are. My father always said, "Be the person you're looking for". Knowing who you are keeps you in your lane. You never see a bird trying to swim like a fish, because the bird knows he was created to fly, therefore, swimming is not an issue with the bird. The bird can never be pressured into ever being fish.

When you really know who you are, there are certain things you are not willing to do. I am reminded of a young lady who went to a club one night. As she was leaving the club, she was jumped by three girls and severely beaten. She wanted revenge. She drove home, got a gun and drove back to the club looking for the three girls. Found them, shot and killed all three of them. Today she is a lifer in the penitentiary. If there was ever a time to put it on pause that was her time. As she drove home, she had time to calm down, and cool off. Driving back to the club she had more time to reconsider her actions and chose not to. The warning signs are there to help us. Our choices are important. Her choice cost her life in prison.

Not all storms in life come to disrupt your life. Sometimes they come to clear your path. Disruptions can be signs to warn you when to put it on pause. Give yourself permission to pause a minute and think before you react. James 1:19 says. "*Be quick to listen, but slow to speak. And be slow to become angry"*. So, I said that to say this, before you send that text, put it on pause, before you take that next drink, put it on pause, before you feel the need to harm yourself or somebody else, please put it on pause.

After we broke up, I realized the school band was not for me. I pursued my music with a passion. You may be a student, a secretary or a nurse, but if you can quit your job today and do something else tomorrow, you have not found your purpose. Your job is what you do, your purpose is what God has called you to do. When you find your purpose, you find who you are and complete fulfillment. If you do not know what your purpose is. Pray and ask God with a sincere heart, then wait patiently for the answer. He promised in 1 John 5:14 NET if we asked anything according to his will, he would hear us and answer us. His will is his word.

Realizing music was the platform God gave me to encourage and inspire others, I was honored. Anytime I find myself singing on a stage whether large or small the audience, I know I am where I am supposed to be. If you want to find your true purpose in life, put it on pause and seek God's word. Jeremiah 29:11 says. *"For I know the plans I have for you, "Declares the Lord, "plans to prosper you and not harm you, plans to give you hope and a future".* I took him at his word.

Today, I am the CEO and Founder of a youth organization entitled, **Yes, I Can Ministries, Inc**. I also host a conference entitled "JUST GIRLS" designed to empower and encourage young women with a message of hope in Jesus Christ. As a singer-songwriter and producer, I have had the opportunity of working with some of the biggest artists in the music business. Like Mickael Jackson, The King of Pop, mega superstar, Whitney Houston, Multi award winning Amy Grant, Stephan Curtis Chapman, Phil Collins, BeBe Winans, Smokey Robinson, and the king of Gospel, Andrea Crouch. My first record, Gospel Reggae, entitled "Amarachi" received international acclaim and was featured in Billboard Magazine as being the hottest music project of the year. My latest single "SWAG" is a tribute to Barack Obama as the First Black President of the United States of America, it crossed over on the Smooth Jazz charts and the video made #1 in the top 10 most favorite watched videos.

When COVID-19 hit our country, my life like so many others was moving at a fast pace. COVID-19 quickly became a world-wide pandemic, I felt fear knocking at my door. The fear was a warning, so I used the stay-at-home time to pray daily. And boy, was that a game changer that allowed me to refocus on what I was doing and why?

Sometimes, with all the Hustle and bustle we tend to stray off course. But God is like the GPS in your car. Once you ask it for direction It will route you to your destination, and if you get off course, as we often do the GPS will patiently reroute you back on course to your destination. Staying in the will of God kind of works the same way. Troubles will always come, James 1:2 says, *"Count it all joy when you meet with trouble"*. 2 Timothy 1:7 says, *"For God has not given you a spirit of fear but power, love and a sound mind"*.

It is never too late to change directions. You can live above your circumstances by the choices you make. So, do not blame God when bad things happen to you. John 10:10 says, "*Satan comes to still, kill, and destroy*". God is the one who will pull you out and protect you from evil. So, I challenge you today, to use the word of God as the yardstick by which we must live our life.

Once I heard a young lady share her story about a guy she had dated. She shared how they went out on dinner dates together, he took her shopping, she even had the keys to his apartment. One day she noticed she was not feeling well and went to the doctor. She was shocked when the doctor told her she had aids. Feeling devastated she called and told her mother. She later found out her boyfriend had knowingly given her aids. Her story was so compelling I invited her to speak at my Just Girls Conference. She gladly accepted. Sadly enough, she passed away before conference time came. Every choice you make will affect your life. So, be good to yourself and pray about everything.

Does a hammer tear down or build up? It is not about the hammer it is what you do with the hammer. So, remember the choices you make today could cost your life tomorrow. So, before you react, PUT IT ON PAUSE!

Born in San Diego, California, *Gail Moore*, is an accomplished pianist, singer, songwriter, and producer. *Singing backup for the King of Pop, Michael Jackson, Whitney Houston, Donna Summer,* *she also hosts a "JUST GIRL'S" conference designed to empower young women.*

Gail is *CEO and Founder of "YES I CAN Ministries, Inc. a youth* *organization b*ringing a message of hope to a hurting world.

Visit her artist website @ www.gailmooremusic.com or email@ gailpmoore@gmail.com

STUDY 1

REFINEMENT TO INFLUENCE

You Are Chosen

"But you are a chosen generation, a royal priesthood, a holy nation, His own special people, that you may proclaim the praises of Him who called you out of darkness into His marvelous light" (1 Peter 2:9, NKJV).

Recommended Readings

"I chose you before I formed you in the womb; I set you apart before you were born. I appointed you a prophet to the nations" (Jeremiah 1:5)

"My grace is sufficient for you, for My strength is made perfect in weakness." Therefore, most gladly I will rather boast in my infirmities, that the power of Christ may rest upon me" (2 Corinthians 12:9, NKJV).

Troubles will always come, James 1:2 says. "*Count it all joy when you meet with trouble*". 2 Timothy 1:7 says, "*For God has not given you a spirit of fear but power, love and a sound mind*".

"Beloved, do not be surprised at the fiery trial when it comes upon you to test you, as though something strange was happening to you..." (1 Peter 4:12, ESV).

"that we were "bought at a price; therefore, we glorify God in body and in spirit, which is God's" (1 Corinthians 6:20, NKJV).

James 1:19 says. "*Be quick to listen, but slow to speak. And be slow to become angry*".

Reflect - What meaning does this provide me, as His chosen one?

_____

_____

_____

_____

_____

_____

_____

_____

_____

_____

_____

_____

_____

_____

_____

_____

_____

_____

Rise Up Chosen One! -

"Get wisdom! Get understanding! Do not forget, nor turn away from the words of my mouth. Do not forsake her, and she will preserve you; Love her, and she will keep you. Wisdom is the principal thing; Therefore, get wisdom. And in all your getting, get understanding" (Proverbs 4:5-7, NKJV).

Individual Questions and Activities

Do you cultivate character strengths of His chosen ones (compassion, kindness, humility, gentleness, patience, forgiving, accepting, peacekeeper, grateful and generous)?

Yes_____ No_____

If your answer is Yes, then...

Complete this sentence - What would you want to be doing, if resources (money etc.) were not a consideration, _____ _____, who would you do it for, _____and for what amount of time_____.

Do you know what your purpose is?

Yes _____ No _____

Write out your purpose.

_____

_____

_____

_____

_____

Action Step - Pray and ask God with a sincere heart, then wait patiently for the answer. He promised in 1 John 5:14 NET if we ask anything according to his will, he will hear us and answer us. His will is his word.

Jeremiah 29:11 says. _"For I know the plans I have for you, "Declares the Lord, "plans to prosper you and not harm you, plans to give you hope and a future"._

It is never too late to change directions. You can live above your circumstances by the choices you make. So, do not blame God when bad things happen to you. John 10:10 says, _"Satan comes to still, kill, and destroy"._ God is the one who will pull you out and protect you from evil. So, I challenge you today, to use the word of God as the yardstick by which we must live life.

Small Group Activities -

1. Are you currently living life by design or by default?

_____

_____

2. If you're living life by default, identify 3-5 things you can do over the next 30 days to get out of the rut and back into alignment with your purpose?

   1. _____
   2. _____
   3. _____
   4. _____
   5. _____

3. Your story lines are important. Think of an experience that surfaces as you are doing this work, write it down. Take some time, then reflect, and see if you can identify themes and patterns. Let your instinct guide you how far back you want to go. For purposes of this exercise, you want the words to flow, so allow yourself to write without editing.

Did you identify any themes or patterns? Please write them down.

_____
_____
_____
_____
_____
_____
_____
_____

Now that you've written your story, re-read it. What lesson(s) did you learn from the experience that could help others? Write those lesson(s) below.

_____

_____

_____

_____

_____

_____

_____

_____

Small Group Discussion

Share with the group one character attribute that you are working on to cultivate within yourself, in order to manifest a heart after Christ.

Request feedback, actively listen, and integrate thoughts without providing a reaction or response. Now take a few minutes, alone, and journal how you are feeling, then take a few cleansing breaths, and write down what action you can take to reconcile others' perceptions and your own, to who God says you are.

_____

_____

_____

_____

_____

PART II

THE UNIQUE DESIGN
OF THE CHOSEN

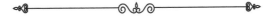

Determined to Rise

By Tiffany Jacobsen

1 Peter 2:9 *"But you are a chosen race, a royal priesthood, a Holy nation, a people for God's own possession that you may proclaim the excellencies of Him who has called you out of darkness and into his marvelous light."*

This was the verse that changed my life after overcoming so much. The fact that HE chose me changed my heart and my mind. NO longer was I the titles the world had given me. no longer was I the victim of circumstances that life had handed to me. I was chosen, I was HIS. Knowing HE chose me gave me a reason to hold onto hope. The very thing that set me free was to know who I was in HIM and that HE accepted and adopted me into HIS family. What he has done for me, HE can do for you.

I went from being told I had no purpose, that I could be bought at a price and was an object for people to use and thrown away afterwards, which made me doubt my worth growing up. I changed into being bought at a price that He paid on the cross that would save my life by HIS amazing love. The price He paid to set me free was more than anything I could have gone through in life. Jesus kept his eyes on the father through everything he walked through, He went through betrayals, scoffing, ridicule, being hated on, even on the cross when He paid a price for us all to be chosen into the kingdom. What amazing love that is, even in our darkest moments He loves us through it. He handpicked us for HIS purpose for such a time as this.

Being a survivor of abuse and trafficking, these truths can be extremely hard to believe at first. The very people that were supposed to love and protect me, my own family chose to walk away, but God adopted me into His family. I started to believe the truth that I was chosen, that I am worthy of HIS amazing love, that HE would want to use me, the me that everyone else threw away and treated me like I was worthless. It is incredibly hard to believe that HE sees me as so precious and priceless to be used by Him, to be a light in the dark world I came out of. I stand in awe of the simple fact that such a BIG God would want to use someone that the rest of the world would see as the least of these. I felt overlooked by family and the world, but the joy in my heart that I was loved, accepted and chosen by HIM!

How awesome is that?

He chose us when the rest of the world had dismissed our very existence. He gives our life purpose again, he gives us hope again when all hope seems lost. That in itself is truly a gift, when so much trauma and rejection takes place in life HE never leaves us where we are at, he gently guides us back to HIM. How he longs for us to know His truth in who we are in HIM.

He helped me overcome so much, because there comes a point in life that you no longer want to live in the definition of what the world has given you. You start believing in His word and truth.

Once that truth gets planted in your heart, it ignites a fire to get up and fight. It gives you a determination to rise above it all and do whatever it takes to stomp out the lies that we believed for so long, and to share with others the truth of who they are called to be. His truth truly sets us apart and sets us free. His truth roots out all the lies that we once so strongly believed, as we start planting HIS word in our hearts and minds in their place. We grow into everything He has called us to be.

Once I started to see HIS truths, I started to see my value and genuinely love myself, which is a big victory, because for years of my life there was no love for self or self-value. I got to a point in my life where enough was enough and that pushed me to the frontlines to stand up and fight. Once you are pushed to the frontlines you gain a tenacity, a fierceness that makes you determined to rise above anything that comes at you in life. You no longer get pushed into being silent or let others instill fear in your heart, you start owning your truth. I started speaking and believing my truth. It was not an easy road to get to, the enemy had many attempts to try and get me to take my own life, BUT GOD stepped in and stomped those thoughts out. Being chosen by him gives hope to keep moving forward. Even if I do not know or see HIS plan, I can trust that I now serve a bigger purpose then what the world has given.

Being chosen by Him can truly be a life changing experience. Once you know and believe that truth you stand firm on that truth and you truly become who you were created to be. He truly does call us out of darkness into HIS marvelous light. It is His light that shines into those dark and shattered pieces of the heart, it is His light that awakens our hearts to HIS. When we begin to believe His truth, the lies we once believed and things that fulfilled us once before becoming uncomfortable, there is a deep yearning in our hearts that something needs to change, and we cannot keep being stuck in those lies or circumstances. This is where the determination to rise above comes into play. Once you know the truth in who you are so many things start changing in your life.

- You start to recognize your worth

- You start setting healthy boundaries

- You start gaining vision for life and start dreaming again

- You start being pickier about who you let into your inner trust circle

- You start filling that void in your heart with HIS word and truth, you wish to spend more time in word and prayers

- All in all, you start making smarter and healthier choices

I spent most of my life living in unworthiness, guilt and shame thinking to myself why God would, see me and choose me. Everyone else threw me away but He picked me up and handpicked me to do HIS will and be adopted into HIS family. He can do the same for you. Choices in life change after you are chosen. You start believing in yourself again, you have value because you start to believe in who he says you are not what you have been told.

Before I knew I was chosen I had made bad choices in life. This girl that everyone thought they could use, and abuse had no worth, no direction. I felt like I had no purpose, I had so many attempts at suicide as a youth and as an adult. Growing up as a girl trafficked and abandoned by family, I truly was hopeless.

There was not a day that went by that I was not praying God please take me away. I looked for love and relationships to fill the void, eventually that led me to abusive relationships which decreased and made me feel even more devalued and more forgetful of HIS truth. By his amazing grace I went from so codependent to my full reliance and filled with him! He filled me with love, and I started learning who I was in HIM, I started being comfortable being alone, and finding out who I truly was without trying to fit into a role others wanted me to be. I was finally free to be me. I now take myself out on dates on beautiful trails just to be alone with the Lord and really listen in the quiet. I was no longer afraid of being on my own. I didn't need anyone to validate me. I value myself a lot more and my standards are set way higher because I know who I am and whose I am. I may have a small circle of people I trust but they value me and encourage me to be all HE has created me to be, and for once in my life I feel worthy to have people in my life. I no longer have to push people out of my life before they can hurt me. God gives me the discernment and has placed people in my life that I know were sent directly from him, this I know because I feel so much peace in my heart and am filled with HIS love when I am around them. Only God can take a broken, guarded girl, into someone that is confident and knows who she is in HIM and no longer settles for just anything. I have worth and I am worthy of respect and love. I could have never said that even a year ago , but I started believing HIS truth and knowing I was chosen gave me the confidence and strength to move forward. HE can and will do the same for you.

So many days I wondered if my family did not want me, then why was I placed on this earth, what Lord is my purpose?

The emptiness inside my heart led to looking for love in wrong places, which led to more abusive relationships and filling the void with everything but HIM, I truly felt so undeserving of HIS love for me. I tried to fit in wherever I could because I truly did not know my own identity, just what I was raised up into and what my abusers had said to me which was far from his truth. This kind of living got old, so many years of feeling this way not knowing and continuing to live in that victim and survival mindset. That is where my determination to rise came in.

I had my breaking point where I said enough is enough. I had enough of being pushed around and bullied by my ex, I had enough of staying silent about being trafficked and the abuse I went through to keep everyone else comfortable. There was a fight inside of me I could not explain, the only way to explain it is God lifting me out of that dark place and igniting my heart to have determination to rise above the situation's life had thrown at me, to rise above the lies that they had said, to rise above the victim mindset into having a mindset of victory to overcome it all. To rise above the survival mode to keep moving forward mode. This truly pushed me forward to the frontlines to stand up and have my voice and start truly finding out who I am in HIM. I no longer need to have validation from relationships or others, because I am validated by the one who chose me and so are you. There is truly freedom in that.

When I finally found my truth and worth in him, it gave me a new boldness to fight for those that have not made it to the point where they are able to get out yet, it gave me a boldness and determination to rise and be a voice for the voiceless, to be HIS heart, hands, and feet. I went from being a hopeless woman to a woman filled with Hope and heart wanting to instill the same hope I had found into the hearts of those without hope, because I overcame that and know what it feels like to be hopeless.

Owning our own truth can be uncomfortable because we are so used to living in the lies from our past, we can no longer live in that bondage, it holds us back from who God has truly called to be, to walk in HIS truth and the HIS freedom in knowing who we are in him. We must choose to have determination to rise above it all and keep fighting to own and speak our truth. We start walking with our heads held a little bit higher the more we walk in the freedom of truth and know that HE has chosen and appointed us for such a time as this to be a voice of boldness.

Being chosen is truly life changing. Of all the years I wasted living with the victim mindset and living in the shackles and chains of the lies and beliefs I had, I was set free, I started to have vision again. I finally started to let people in my life. People that HE specifically placed in my life to remind me of who I am in HIM because yes, there are many days I forget.

When you have believed the lies for so long, it takes time to retrain your brain. I have friends that remind me of who and whose I am. I started to unbury the dreams I had buried deep years ago, because at the time there was just no opportunity to pursue my dreams, I was too busy surviving. Now I am busy thriving to unfold and unbury the dreams HE had placed in my heart to do. Inspired by someone that truly means the world to me. We sat in the dirt in the middle of her horse paddock and sat in silence and she talked to me about what God wanted to remind me of and it was the dreams that I buried. That day changed the course of my whole life. I started dreaming again no matter how impossible it looks or is, with HIM ALL things are possible. I started praying and asking HIM to remind me of all the dreams I had buried that HE had placed in my heart. I started taking action, they say faith without works is dead and it is so very true. We can say we have the faith but HE gives us the steps we need to take, we can choose to sit on the steps or get up and start stepping up and moving forward in faith and consistently seek him in guidance in ALL we do. Be prayerful about every step and take the time to be still enough to listen, sometimes he makes us wait and other times it feels like he pushes us forward. Staying focused on him while taking these steps is so imperative.

I am starting to act on what I need to do to carry out the vision I have. Even as I am sitting here writing, this was part of my dream to share and speak my truth and pray it gives hope to someone that needs to hear it. I am going to school to do equestrian ministry as my dream is to have my own ranch someday so I can help others through the trauma and hopelessness and bring hope

54

and healing through horses and healing. Just this very weekend I received my Equine Trauma Therapy certificate, one step closer to my goal, an action and work I had to do to move forward in the direction of the dreams he has for me.

Please never give up on your dreams, I am telling you it's worth it. Keep moving forward, I am living proof. I am now gaining the courage to speak, this will be the first year I will be doing public speaking, I am very introverted so I know it will be HIM that speaks through me and HIM that will give me the strength and boldness to do so. I stepped out of my comfort zone also this weekend and did a photo shoot with some amazing warriors to raise awareness for sex trafficking, we had to choose words to write on our arms that would give a message, mine were fight back by owning truth and being silent no longer and the other one was be fearless and move forward in boldness truth. Being fearless helps us be more determined to rise. As survivors HE gives the strength to do just that. No more being fearful we have courage and boldness that comes directly from HIM.

I could have not done any of this without knowing and finally owning my truth. My heart is after you read this, I pray it encourages you to go deeper and find your truth. You are no longer the messages of your past or a victim of your circumstances, you are a true warrior chosen by HIM. Own that truth and get that determination to rise above it. All the lies, the betrayals, the abuse, the molestation, the financial situation, whatever it is, you too can rise above it all. How awesome is it that HE chose you as his warrior for the kingdom?! Life changing, right?! Absolutely, I am so determined to rise that I am driven to want to learn tactical training for self defense so I can teach other women and survivors self defense and share how I overcame and what pushed me into the determination to rise above and fight back. That in itself only HE can do because I used to be so passive and ashamed to stand up for self. HE can do the same for you, I am a living testimony.

What dreams have you buried deep down that you cannot remember?

Will you rise above the self-doubt and circumstances, and start digging those dreams back up?

Take the action you need to achieve them. He put the dreams and vision in your heart, but you need to take the steps of faith and action. I pray after reading this, you too will have the determination to rise.

Take some time to just sit in silence and hear what HE has placed inside of you. You are chosen to be a light in the darkness. Surround yourself with people that will encourage and inspire you to keep moving forward in the direction of your dreams. When you feel like quitting, reach out and keep your eyes on HIM.

What lies are you still believing now?

I challenge you to replace each lie with a word of HIS truth and read it daily to yourself until you start to believe it. I still do that to this day.

What obstacles do you need to overcome the dream he has placed in your heart?

I pray you get the boldness and determination to rise above anything that tries to come in the way of you achieving it. HE chose you, now it is time for you to choose you too. You are fearfully and wonderfully made. You are worthy to be chosen, you are worthy to pursue your dreams, you are worthy to own your truth.

I pray my story encourages and inspires you into a determination to rise above. If God can take someone like me and use me, HE is no respecter of persons, HE chose you for a purpose. (Jeremiah 29:11-13). We are no longer a victim of circumstances or the lies told to us. We are CHOSEN by HIM, warriors that are determined to rise above and keep moving forward into all that he called us to be. It is time to rise and rise above, others are depending on your story so they can have some hope.

Be bold, be fearless, live life with tenacity with a true determination to rise above it all and own your truth, speak your truth.

Onward mighty warrior this is your season to rise!

Just keep putting one foot in front of the other and continue to take the steps of faith and act and watch God do the rest!

Dream again, live again, do not quit, keep moving forward!

You are Chosen by HIM! This is reason enough to keep going.

Tiffany Jacobsen is a single mother who grew up in the small town of Medford Wisconsin. She is a first time author and also a public speaker. She has a passion for justice and raising awareness for domestic violence and trafficking as she has personally survived it herself. She is driven to be a voice to the voiceless, to encourage and empower women that have gone through and been through it. She truly believes that with God and people coming alongside those that are hurting can make a difference in the lives of those that are and have been affected.

Tiffany's goal is to inspire and give hope to those that are hurting. She has a strong faith in God that she truly lives by, her desire is to be God's heart, hands and feet in the community and be a voice of hope. She enjoys the outdoors and spending time with her son. She uses what she has overcome to encourage others that they can overcome too. She loves to be a light in a dark world. She has a heart to serve. She believes that no matter what you go through, with God on your side you can overcome and is truly passionate about making others see the fighter in themselves.

God will always get the glory for the story. Willing to go to the frontlines to fight for justice. Truly believes if each person steps out in boldness in their faith, we can be world changers. Be HIS ♥ heart.

Email: Warriorsarise31@gmail.com
Personal web page coming soon.

Stand Uncovered from Shame: You are Free

by Angel Carter

True freedom is being uncovered in the face of shame! That means I can tell my story and uncover my secrets because I have been set free from shame. I'm no longer bound, and I can face that shame by exposing it for what it is and not receiving it as my own.

"Therefore, if the son makes you free, you shall be free indeed" (John 8:36, NKJV).

I never imagined as a child I would have to face so much adversity and loneliness. My whole life, I felt different from everyone else, the way I looked, the way I dressed, the way I walked. I always wanted to fit in with the popular crowd. I would have done just about anything to be liked by others and to be accepted. Here is where the lie of never being good enough first germinated in my mind. I began to create a fantasy world, a world that people would accept, a version of myself that I wanted to be. My dad had passed away when I was five years old, so we did not have much financially growing up.

My mother did the best she could in keeping us in clothes and shoes for school; that is when I realized I did not dress like everyone else. I remember daydreaming all the time wishing I were like the other girls prettier, popular, and normal. I felt like I was none of these things and could not understand why I was so different from others or why my family could not be like other families. The church was my escape from reality, my grandfather was a Pastor, and my whole family played an instrument or sang in the choir. I remember loving going to church with my grandfather, who was so kind and gentle. I still giggle when I think about his perfect comb over blowing in the wind on our Sunday morning rides to church. He was indeed a man of faith and loved Jesus. He mirrored his love so wonderfully, and everyone that knew my grandfather experienced a glimpse of heaven.

When he passed away, we stopped going to church, and that is when the darkness showed up, and incest had introduced itself to me for the first time. It did not show up angered or forceful, it was smooth-talking and persuasive, making me submissive, feeling that I was in the wrong, and I should feel guilty for not giving in to its masked demands. By the time I was ten years old, my purity and identity had been stolen; I could not outrun this darkness; it was etched in my very soul; it followed me like my own shadow. When you are a child, you are pure and innocent; you should not have to think about protecting your purity; hide and seek was supposed to be a fun game, but not in my world. When I hid, it was to protect myself from saying yes to things I did not want to do. My family, like many others, is full of dark secrets of abuse, addiction, incest, and many other ungodly patterns of sin; sin is a hungry cycle that never gets satisfied. It travels from one generation to the next, destroying everything and everyone in its path. It has no compassion, only a vicious taste for souls.

The scriptures read in Deuteronomy 5:9-10 You shall not bow down to them nor serve them. For I, the Lord your God, am a jealous God, visiting the iniquity of the fathers upon the children to the third and fourth generations of those who hate me, but showing mercy to thousands, to those who love me and keep my commandments.

"I call heaven and earth as witnesses today against you that I have set before you life and death, blessing and cursing; therefore, choose life, that both you and your descendants may live"(Deuteronomy 30:19,NKJV).

That means choosing to do what is right instead of what is wrong. My family continued to choose the wrong path even though they knew the right way; My family, both on my mother and my father's side, grew up in church, my grandfathers were pastors, so they knew God's commandments and yet chose to defile them, leaving traces of curses, trauma, and pain along the way for the next generation to suffer. As I tasted this bitter cup, I would punish myself by hating who I was. I would think the most horrible, disgusting thoughts about myself. The darkness so blinded me I did not want to live; I would constantly cut myself, sometimes it was because I wanted to die and other times, I just wanted relief, and each time that I reached death's door, somehow life would grab me and sustain me until the next time my soul surrendered to the blade. The shame that I felt was exhausting; it felt like I was in a constant tug, a war between the shame of allowing myself to participate in such ungodliness and the guilt of keeping it a secret so that no one could judge me.

I was emotionally and mentally bound to this darkness most of my life. As the years passed, this destructive cycle continued to wreak havoc through my bloodline, taking away everything I ever loved. I was trying to fill the emptiness that I felt with drugs, alcohol, and sex. I had four beautiful children by different fathers adding on more shame on top of what was already there. I watched my family slowly fall apart as we began to lose loved ones, my uncle, and then my baby sister. My pain was only growing deeper and darker. I believed I could fill the void with love, so I got married, hoping that love would heal my heart. Wrong again, I was broken and damaged. I could not genuinely love someone else when I could not love myself. Out of four of my kids, I only had two living with me, my daughters, and my stepson.

My children watched my destructive patterns as I struggled to live. When your children see addiction, loss, and trauma, it is bound to affect them somehow. My youngest daughter Alexis started to face those same demons I and my brothers and sister did. She went from this sweet little girl to this depressed teenager. She was sneaking out, doing drugs, and skipping school. I had no idea how to help her because I could not help myself. This lifestyle led her to be raped, abused, exploited, and then left for dead. This was when my heart took its last attempt to fail on me, but somehow it was still beating, very painfully. I felt shame, guilt, and so much pain I never thought I would be ok, that my life was just meant to suffer. I lost everything and everyone. I was at rock bottom. I was afraid, but I needed help.

So, I hit my knees; I could not live, I could not die, all I could do was call out to the name of Jesus and hope that he would save me.

"For whoever calls on the name of the Lord shall be saved"(Romans 10:13,NKJV).

Not only did He save me, but He gave me a new life and plan through surrender. First, I needed to get sober, and I could not do it independently, so I went into an addiction treatment center and began the process of grieving and healing. Looking back as I tell my story, I am filled with gratitude that I am not where I used to be. I am free, and if I can be free from my trauma and pain, you can be too. Healing is one of the most important, beautiful, attainable, achievable gifts you could ever give yourself.

It is essential to go through the process of grieving your past. The trauma and the pain of your past will manifest in one negative form or another. For example, if someone betrayed you and you do not correctly grieve and heal from that betrayal, it will always show up in your relationships and friendships; you will never truly trust anyone, not even yourself. That keeps your heart hardened and closed off, so when the honest and authentic relationships come along, you will not perceive them as real but as false, and you reject the very thing your heart longs for. So, you see, it is essential to heal from our wounds and losses to receive all that God has for us.

I had to begin to untangle the web of shame, guilt, lies, and torment that I have been entangled with my whole life to receive healthy relationships and become teachable. Once I realized that I was not at fault, then I was able to begin my process of getting out of the tangled mindset that shame belonged to me.

"Instead of your shame you shall have double honor and instead of confusion, they shall rejoice in their portion. Therefore, in their land, they shall possess double; Everlasting joy shall be theirs" (Isaiah 61:7, NKJV).

My healing journey has been imperfectly perfect. I had to be patient with myself and others, allowing myself room to grow, which means making mistakes along the way and learning from one another. Forgiveness was a huge part of my healing. I had so much hate toward myself, going over the things I could have or should have done,

Eventually, I decided I wanted life, love, and forgiveness more than I wanted death, hate, and unforgiveness. Transgenerational trauma leaves many warning signs along its trail of destruction. Get to know yourself and your children, find out what is hidden under the surface. Stop the dysfunctional cycle in your family and bloodline. God is our father, and He wants us to come to Him and bring all our heavy, painful burdens so that we can begin the process of healing. The words "Come to the Father" were hard for me to hear at the beginning of my healing journey. I did not have a loving father growing up, and when I thought of a father, I did not see love and protection; I saw perversion, rejection, and abandonment. How could I love the heavenly father and seek to know him if my view was tainted? So when people would say that my father in heaven loves me, I could not see him as pure. I wanted to, but my thoughts had been twisted, and my eyes blinded for so long that I did not know a father-daughter bond. I had to be honest with myself and God; that was how I felt, and that my thoughts toward Him were not good.

One day I was sitting at church, and after the service, people were walking around praying for one another, and I was sitting alone, just crying out to God, releasing the pain that had surfaced to the top of my heart. A sweet lady sat down beside me, praying for me, then she began to sing over my heart, and at that time, a little child ran down the aisle and fell. A man came rushing for him and picked him up and said it's ok daddies got you and the lady sitting next to me said, that's how your father in heaven feels about you, and at that very moment, it was like a wrecking ball had broken through the wall that was around my mindset of a father. That was what a real father does; he picks us up and comforts us when we fall or get hurt in any way. That was the beginning of my journey to understand the father's heart toward me. I have to remind myself often of these memories because those destructive and unwanted thoughts that made their way in my mind would try to come back and discourage me, so I replaced them with new memories.

If our father's perception is off and we do not know God's real identity, then we cannot know who we indeed are. We are all children of God, and sometimes our view of the father can be skewed. Some may have never had a father; some have had a father who abused them, physically, sexually, or emotionally. That separates the father-daughter, father-son bond, which can leave you feeling unloved, rejected, abandoned, and even angry, creating unforgiveness. Whatever the situation, it is hard to view a father in a loving, acceptable, and kind way.

If you have experienced any of these things or things that were not listed. I want to say I am so sorry for what you have endured.

There is a heavenly father that wants to love you with pure love and heal the wounds in your heart.

"For I know the thoughts that I think toward you, says the Lord, thoughts of peace and not of evil, to give you a future and a hope" (Jeremiah 29:11, NKJV).

You may even have to forgive God the Father because you feel he wasn't there when these things happened to you. He was always there; he collected every tear.

"You number my wanderings; Put my tears into Your bottle; Are they not in Your book?" (Psalm 56:8, NKJV).

You are a valuable treasure to God; in fact, he loves you so much that he sent his son Jesus Christ to die for you, your sin, your pain, and your shame.

"For God so loved the world that He gave His only begotten Son, that whoever believes in Him should not perish but have everlasting life" (John 3:16, NKJV).

Imagine someone taking a bullet for you, dying in your place. Well, that's precisely what Jesus did for you and me. He took our shame and sin with Him on the cross, and now we can be free from our past. I invite you to make the most important decision of your life and invite Jesus into your heart and ask God to forgive all your sins and experience the freedom of being a son or daughter.

"I say to you that likewise there will be more joy in heaven over one sinner who repents than over ninety-nine just persons who need no repentance" (Luke 15:7,NKJV).

God will repay those who have done evil to you. It is ok to release them now. Take the first step of healing today and release those who have harmed you, give them to Jesus. Lord, I pray in the name of Jesus Christ that whoever is reading this will be brave and courageous and will release anyone that they have unforgiveness toward and that you would heal the wound and pain of where that unforgiveness lived in their heart, and that they would know that vengeance belongs to you.

"Beloved, do not avenge yourselves, but rather give place to wrath; for it is written, "Vengeance is Mine, I will repay," says the Lord" (Roman's 12:19,NKJV).

Nothing happens by mistake, you are **CHOSEN!**

" But you are the ones chosen by God, chosen for the high calling of priestly work, chosen to be a holy people, God's instruments to do his work and speak out for him, to tell others of the night-and-day difference he made for you—from nothing to something, from rejected to accepted" (1Peter 2:9,10,MSG).

May the Lord bless you and your children and your children's, children's.

"The Lord bless you and keep you; The Lord make His face shine upon you And be gracious to you; The Lord lift up His countenance upon you, And give you peace" (Numbers6:24-26,NKJV).

Born in South Carolina, Angel Carter is the CEO of Angel of Revelations Deliverance Ministry. Her story is one of traversing through many tragedies and terrible misfortunes that a young woman should never have had to endure. Angel's family history is one riddled with physical abuse, sexual deviance, mental illness, witchcraft, and substance abuse all of which affected her childhood and life in some way.

Angel found herself caught in the snares of incest through sexual abuse as a child, addiction to medications as an adult and tormented by generational bondage's revisiting her through doors opened by prior generations in her bloodline. She struggled to find her identity which had been distorted and broken by the influences that were trying to define her.

But God had another plan. Out of her own darkness of abuse into His marvelous light, Angel was thrust into purpose after her daughter's tragic demise to the grips of abuse, addiction, and sexual exploitation that seemed to plague her life and now that of her children. God used a painful circumstance to work for her good, because it was then that Angel garnered strength, courage, and fortitude to stand up to Satan's bullying tactics, and demanded reparations for all that had been stolen, including her identity.

Today, Angel's passion is to bring truth and light to those who have lost their identity to the enemy's lies, tricks and schemes because she, herself once felt like a face without a name. She uses the Word to be a lamp unto her feet, as a highly skilled leader, woman of purpose and demon chaser. She is a powerhouse of faith that has overcome the world by reliance on the blood of the lamb and the word of her testimony. Angel now understands, believes, and lives the scriptural text in Jeremiah 29:11, "for I know the plans I have for you," says the LORD. "They are plans for good and not for disaster, to give you a future and a hope. "Amen

To contact Angel,please go to:

Email:angelcofrevelations@gmail.com
Phone:(561)397-6880
Facebook: Angel Carter

Out of the night,
I chose me

by Wendy L. Elliott

I was free, running to my safety, yelling and knocking on doors for help! It was late at night and no one was showing signs of being awake, no one was answering their doors or my cries for help. I could not stay at one door for very long because I knew **he** would be coming after me.

After turning around to look over my shoulder I saw him, I also very clearly saw one of our large kitchen knives in his hand. He was yelling for me to come back and that he would not hurt me. Why would I believe that? I thought for a second, "He won't hurt me" then I remembered what brought me outside in the dark just a few minutes earlier, now running for my life. I realized that in the state he was in anything was possible. For one moment as he held me in the choke hold and I fell to the ground appearing to not breathe, he became human again, he had become concerned that he had suffocated me and released the hold to go call 911 leaving me alone on the floor. I thought this was my escape, it was just enough time for me to get up, get to the back door and leave the duplex to my safety. He quickly noticed and had realized that I had tricked him into thinking I was not breathing and was now even more determined to come after me. I wasn't sure if it was the drugs or anger or both, but I definitely didn't want to be caught at that point.

I will call him "T". I met T after a significant breakup for me, I was about to graduate with my master's and start a new life. My boyfriend at the time and I were getting pretty serious and had even talked about getting engaged and married. I thought we were on the same page of wanting to expand our lives outside of Huntington, WV. I had dreams of heading south where it was warmer and greener with much more opportunity. He on the other hand wanted to stay close to his family and join his father in a sales career. Needless to say, we broke up. Broke up hard to where he and his family ended up hating me for years to come. We are now friends on social media and have reconciled our emotions as we have both grown and become what we were meant to be.

I was excited to move forward and have fun as a soon to be college graduate with her entire world to be molded and expressed, but I was scared at the same time. In my dreams I was with a partner that would be able to experience that alongside me. I was scared to "be alone." Growing up in rural West Virginia, most of the girls in my senior class were already married with babies on the way. I knew that God had a different plan for me, but was still scared to leave the only place I ever knew and into the wild world that awaited me. My mom and I had lived alone, in Ranger for greater than 14 years after my daddy passed away at the young age of 48 from a heart attack, so I never really experienced anything or anywhere else.

My girlfriends and I were out one night at one of the busy night clubs where a lot of the college kids hung out and danced. I noticed "T" immediately when I got up to the door, he was tall, muscular, tan, with blonde hair and blue eyes which was exactly what I thought I needed. He was one of the bouncers, friends with the one usually there that we knew quite well. Those big blue eyes pierced through me and I immediately fell head over heels. This was just what I needed to get over my breakup. I did not realize then how this seemingly innocent encounter would impact my life forever.

Thinking back on this today and realizing what I was soon to encounter, I have come to understand that there is a plan for us, maybe unseen at the time, but definitely a plan. We have to, at whatever point in time we have the epiphany, utilize that moment to be intentional in our lives and use that to lead with significance. We don't always know how our stories will end; however, we always have the ability to change the narrative if we so choose.

I have never felt that my story was important, that it would make any difference in anyone's life, always feeling others stories were far more impactful and how could I have a story of impact after hearing the others? I never fully understood or at least ever admitted to myself or anyone else that I had been in a domestic violence relationship. It was only a few occurrences and he never really ended up hurting me. I removed myself from that situation, I just thought it was another milestone in my life just like learning to drive a car, or cooking lasagna. No big deal. However, looking back, it had impacted my life significantly especially as to how I prepared for it never to happen again.

What I had not realized until recently is that my story matters, my story has significance to not just me but to those that hear it. Being in healthcare and in the non-profit world working with survivors of human trafficking and exploitation, I have heard horrendous stories of life threatening, life debilitating and just down right unbelievable experiences that there were no comparisons to the small things that happened to me. How could I even feel that what had happened to me could even be worth telling, what would it do for anyone? How could my stories be of value?

Then it hit me. Helping others tell their story was something I have come to love, helping them have a voice was exhilarating. Seeing how it was healing them from their traumas was insightful. I remember the first time I helped someone find their voice, or at least helped them communicate their needs. I was in grade school. One of my classmates had an articulation disorder and was very difficult to understand. For some reason I wanted to spend time with him and get to where I understood what he was saying then be able to interpret for him if he needed it. At that time, I didn't know what my life or career path was to be, that not only was I to become a communication specialist but that I would help others tell their story and use their voices for healing in a multitude of manners.

So why am I ready to tell my stories now? Because I have finally realized it allows me to show intentionality instead of just living my life. Not only have I figured out that my stories may help others but I want and need to write the story as I live it, so jumping into my life was important, seeing how each and every day and point in time can be a story that potentially helps others in one way or another would help me live that life of significance I so desired.

Everyone loves a good story. They inspire, they connect us to others, they trigger emotions and they give us hope. We have the ability to show humor, excitement, sometimes sadness and trauma but no matter what it is about we only want one thing. We want to matter and have our stories be significant in others lives. Potentially helping others that hear those stores release their pain as well.

I have made many jokes about how many lives or seasons I have had and have literally compartmentalized them as if they didn't all complete or add up to who I am today. I would occasionally describe occurrences in my life to friends or family or even coworkers when it felt it would have some impact on where they were or maybe help them get through some of the things going on in their lives, or to just see how it felt to say out loud.

I had been living in the day and not realizing that how I got here mattered just as much as being here. One of my favorite movies is "It's a Wonderful Life". If you remember the story, George Bailey believes that no one would miss him if he were never born, however with the help of an angel named Clarence, he realized that he had made a difference, he had lived a life where others were positively impacted, a life of significance in which would not have mattered or happened if he never existed.

Now those of you that do know me, you know I do not like to write...I know that is funny since I have been writing almost my entire adult life, two master's degrees, many clinical articles, strategic plans, and yes, several books in the mix, but I have just never felt comfortable or actually felt that I have known what to write about. I have just recently realized that I have to put myself in the story. I have also realized that I am the author of my own life as well. I do not have to physically write my story every day, but I do have to live it and be intentional in what I am doing so that the story going forward is one that I have a say in, that I can plan and be an active participant in.

So, back to my story. I never intended for it to be anything but a pre-graduation fling to get me through the breakup, however that was not the plan. All I really knew about him was that he worked for his dad who was an accountant and that he was in school. He worked at the club part time to just have some fun. Time passed and even though there were red flags, I ignored them and continued the relationship thinking that it would be over soon anyway so, why not? We were enjoying ourselves. I then got a great job in North Carolina and was graduating soon. What would I do?

I never intended for him to move with me to North Carolina where I got my first job, but he did..., I never intended to marry him, but I did.....All choices that I made, maybe out of convenience and not wanting to have a confrontation, or maybe out of the fear of being alone, who knows. Maybe I thought that I needed someone to choose me to be complete. I did not realize at that time that I could have chosen myself....I did not need someone else to choose me to be whole.

Being able to leave WV and have a very successful career had status. Everyone would think I had it made. Getting out of the country, having a college education, getting jobs in great vacation spots with ongoing progression in responsibility and visibility and the ability to move from coast to coast in the process had merit. How could I change the story on them, they all thought I was perfect and had the perfect life to show for it? Although those were the comments that I received and cherished, I felt the need to do more, to continue to be someone worthy of such accolades. This was something that I had strived to be as an overachiever all my life, I was always reaching to be perfect, to show my parents that I was worth them adopting me, choosing me and giving me a wonderful life. How could I disrupt that belief and tell anyone what had really happened to me? I made bad choices, I didn't choose me, I chose to not be in my story.

So, what I did was kick this little occurrence and others out of existence, and just decided to make a plan of what I needed to do to make sure my story was continuing to be a success. Silencing the fear of it recurring, the embarrassment that I had allowed it to happen in the first place and make a new story that didn't include anyone that was ever physically abused by her husband.

It has taken me over 35 years to allow this story to be heard. Why now? Now is the time that I have learned that my story does not define who I am but molds who I have become. When once again I think of George Bailey, I have never allowed others to know the real me, to know that I have experiences that may be helpful to them or that have hurt me. If I look at my life as George did with Clarence, I think that I have impacted others many times and maybe not even noticed it.

I am sorry that I was not present for that part of my story. I love helping others and my lifelong career shows that, but not knowing how much I have had the opportunity to impact others has been a deficit in my life. How many other times have I not been a part of my story? I didn't have the strength nor belief in myself to use my story to live a life of significance.

A desire to live a life of significance doesn't mean I want to be famous, be a saint or get rich monetarily it just means that I want to make a difference to others as well as myself. I just have to believe that I can. I often pull from the story of Ester in the Bible. God uses ordinary people to do extraordinary things; With God's help we can step out in our faith and fight our fears and know that our past does not dictate our future. God places mentors in our lives to teach us wisdom and that we just have to believe we have the ability to make an impact for generations to come.

How the story ended that night is not as important as that **"my story"** continued, not just segments of what happened to me, but **MY STORY,** all of it which made me who I am today. My story of significance and the choices I made have the biggest meaning that **I CHOOSE ME!!!** If you want to know more just ask!!! I am not afraid anymore to talk about who I really am.

5 ways to being the author of your own story of Significance

1) Put yourself in the story

You can paint your story by living it, do not allow it to happen to you. Set your goals and intentions on a regular basis and allow yourself check points as to how you're doing. Redefine, switch up or completely change as you see fit because you can. You can always elaborate and embellish your story afterwards but what would it feel like to live it first?

2) Have Intendment in your story

When we are in intention, we are being intentional in what we do in our lives. We may have to do things we fear or feel are too difficult. If we do not face what we fear it will never change. We need to have a plan. Those that know me know that I use the phrase **"Plan the work and work the plan"**. That's not only for business purposes, that is for our lives. We have to take chances, and sometimes make the wrong choices, but that is not always a bad thing. Do not allow the fear of failing stop you from leading a life of intention.

3) Put your talents, heart and resources in your story

a. You have talents that maybe no one else does so use them to make a difference in someone else's life. You are the only one that can make a difference your way.

b. What is your passion, how does your heart come into play, passion is the fuel so use it to propel what your heart tells you to do?

c. We all have tools in our back pocket, whether it is a memory, a person, a book, use those to be intentional with other's needs.

4) Just do it

When we use words like "I will try" or "I wish I could", or "Hopefully I can get to it" you are not being an active participant in your life. You are using words of good intentions, not of being intentional. When we have good intentions and never act on them, we are not living in our story, we are just wishing we did.

5) Find your Why

Ask yourself how you can add value to others. What makes you sad, happy, lay awake at night, or what do you dream about? All of those things contribute to why you need to tell your story to others and how you can author your own life of purpose to help others. What is the core of who you are? Write all of those down and follow the road map to see where it takes you.

What I have learned is that **it is my story**, my ability to share my experiences with others that may need a bit of encouragement or shine the light as to what I have done to make sure I am present in my story. What happens doesn't define me, it's just a chapter in my life, it is just one page in a very long book and the good part is that I get to write the next chapter.

You also need to realize that you are the artist of your own story, it is up to you to write it with intention and purpose as to your why. Because at the end of the day, if you can stand in your choices and understand why you made them you can tell your story of significance and bestow guidance and triumph as to who you are and why you were chosen to be here.

Wendy Elliott is a corporate executive in healthcare, a successful business entrepreneur with multiple advanced degrees and over two decades of experience in neuroscience and behavioral health healthcare management, executive corporate development and startup businesses. She is a multiple bestselling author and John Maxwell success coach and speaker.

As a well-respected leader and influencer in her profession, Wendy has taken her achievement mentality to exceptional levels in all she does. Wendy is a true believer that you can be on the corporate ladder, as well as have an entrepreneurial spirit. Wendy empowers others to, **"Plan the work and work the plan,"** to overcome all obstacles and obtain one's passion-driven goals.

Throughout her career, she received awards for innovation and thinking outside the box. Wendy focuses on the impact of leadership on engagement and business performance, top team effectiveness, leadership capability development, and talent management strategies.

Wendy is co-founder of **The Elite Foundation** 501(c)(3) non-profit that works to "Fund Freedom" for exploited women, children and other survivors of Human Trafficking and sexual exploitation, Assistant Vice President **of the Marcus Neuroscience Institute at Boca Raton Regional Hospital and** Founder and CEO **of Business Lynx** a consulting company that provides a platform to connect entrepreneurs with executive leadership to achieve high levels of success.

Wendy's goal is to take what she has learned throughout her career and coach/teach others how to use their exceptional talents and God given gifts to get what they want out of life.

You can reach Wendy through LinkedIn, Facebook and Instagram.

Unmasked
It's okay, not to be okay.

by Juliza Kramer

Have you ever felt like life is passing you by? Have you ever woken up and felt like you have no idea what your purpose is in life? I am here to tell you that you are not alone. There have been many occasions in my life when I asked myself what is next? I feel that life is going by and another year has come, and I have accomplished absolutely nothing that I thought I would accomplish by now.

I believe this is a very common way to feel for many people. Hence, the midlife crisis? Growing up I was always the golden child. I got good grades in school, played sports, participated in extracurricular activities, and never got in trouble. I was the 'good kid'. I checked all the boxes. I was given praise and accolades and I thought I knew exactly how to manage life. Upon graduating college from the University of Florida (Go Gators!). I got a job and started my career in marketing.

I prospered quickly. I was ambitious, hungry, a perfectionist. I was in management at a young age and had made it a goal to become a director by the age of thirty, but I did it at the age of twenty-two. I was managing a staff of twenty to fifty employees at any given time. I thought to myself, now what? I hit my goals.

Back to the drawing board. Fast forward to what I believed to be the height of my career, exactly one year ago today. At the age of thirty, I found myself in a wonderful role, with great connections, attending the best social events in town and a relationship that was leading to marriage...so I thought. Everything seemed to be going right. To the outside world, my life was perfect. What I did not realize is that it was all about to come crashing down and I was going to be unmasked.

Our world experienced a global pandemic we all now know as COVID-19. It is crazy how life can change from one minute to the next, right? Even in a split second, your life could drastically change forever. What seemed to be a perfect life came tumbling down. I lost my job; I broke off my romantic relationship and I thought I was going to lose my house and everything I had worked for my entire life. For the first time in my adulthood, I found myself in a place of complete uncertainty. In the beginning, I disappeared from the world. I went into hiding like a hermit crab. Most people would say I fell off the face of the planet. I felt like a failure. And I wanted absolutely no one to know of my failures.

I was known as the woman who had it all together. I have always been successful at reaching my goals. I always look the part and am well put together. I never ask for help and get things done prior to the due date. I meet and exceed goals. I work hard and make my career my life. How could I possibly let anyone into my struggles or pain? Why would I ever allow people to see my vulnerabilities?

Ever heard that life is about timing? I believe that to be true because I believe in a higher power. I believe everything will happen in His timing, not mine. However, I tend to like to be in control so I learned this the hard way. It's all His timing. I've learned to let go, and let God. I know that my Father in heaven, The Creator of all things, knows every hair on my head and every request I am about to make before I make it. I do believe that God's timing is everything in life, but I also believe that we have to live intentionally and listen to the soft still voice of God in order to live out our purpose.

I have been ambitious since I was a little girl. I started working at a young age because I had no other choice. My mother got divorced from my father when I was young, and she had been a housewife her entire life up until that point. She struggled to provide but somehow, I always had everything. I believe God was by our side every step of the way. I made a promise to myself and to her without telling her, that I would succeed and that the struggles we had been through in my younger years would not define my future. Yet here I was thirty-one years old and experiencing emotions that I had experienced in my past. The feeling of abandonment, failure, loneliness, just feeling unequivocally scared. This perfect life that I had created crumbled before my eyes and for the first time since my childhood, I felt empty and without purpose.

The worst part is I isolated myself. I told no one about what was happening or how I was feeling. I did not want people to see me as less than who I thought I was. The truth is it was a lot to handle. It was a lot for anyone to handle. I have since learned the most traumatic losses a human being can experience; 1) death of a loved one 2) divorce 3) moving 4) major illness or injury 5) job loss. Within a year, I experienced ALL these traumatic events that could happen to a person in their life.

I lost a loved one and brought myself a lot of pain by breaking things off with him because I did still love him when I made the decision. I just did not know how to handle all the turmoil happening in my life and I did not know where all the emotions were stemming from. I had to move out of my house because I ended up renting it so that I would not lose it. I caught COVID-19 and had no health insurance anymore to care for myself. And I lost my job. All this happened within a few months starting exactly one year ago.

As you can imagine, I felt hopeless. The pieces of my mask so well constructed through success started to crack. But this is also when I started learning that it's okay to need help and it's okay to not be okay.

Had I not gone through all these trials, hardships, and tribulations I cannot say I would be writing this today. I cannot say this story would have gotten to you. I believe that we are all CHOSEN. We are chosen to live out a purpose greater than what we could ever dream of, think of, or imagine! The problem is that a lot of times we do not see, understand, or come to know our purpose and live it out because we see our setbacks, as failures, and we give up.

I will admit to you that there were a few times throughout the past year I gave up. I wanted nothing to do with all the pain, hurt, heartbreak, and struggles. But what I was reminded of is that we all must break in order to come back much stronger and learn life lessons. Think about it like this, if your life is always perfect and you experience no pain, no struggle, no heartbreak, you start to take life for granted. Don't we all? I am guilty of this myself. It took my entire life falling apart to come to the realization that there were areas in my life I needed to change, and I needed to grow. I would have never admitted this a year ago. I did not have the ability to. I have learned to let the mask come off. It has been a process and you can get there too.

What if I told you that your failures are locking you up for everything you are meant to do and be? What if I told you that there is purpose in your pain? Often, we tell ourselves lies such as "I'm a failure." "I missed my chance." "My life is over." Sound familiar? Trust me, I have been there. We throw a pity party feeling sorry for ourselves and giving up on the aspirations, goals, and dreams we have set before us.

What I am now here to tell you on the other side of all the pain is that – YOU ARE CHOSEN!

You are CHOSEN to live out your purpose. A purpose that was uniquely created by a Master Creator specifically and perfectly tailored to you! YOU, my friend, have a story to tell and gifts to share with the world.

You know what? I have good news and I have bad news for you. Which would you like first?

Let us start with the bad news. The bad news is that you will experience pain in life. It is inevitable. We all have problems. We will all go through struggles and we will all suffer. No one's life is perfect. No one. However, what sets apart the ones who fulfill their purpose in life from the ones who do not is that they learn from their mistakes, pain, and struggles. Every painful situation you have ever been through is an opportunity to learn and grow.

I would say that if you are sitting here reading this today, you may be going through a difficult season of life. You may have just lost your job as I did. You may be having relationship issues or be enduring a breakup or divorce. You or a loved one could be experiencing health issues or maybe your business is failing. Whatever it is that you are struggling with, keep your chin up and your head held high. Be confident in knowing that you are chosen with intentionality by God to fulfill a purpose that you have not even discovered yet! And this season you are going through, feeling depressed, uncertain, scared, hurt, betrayed, or any other emotion you are feeling is forcing you to grow. You are growing in wisdom, maturity, and emotional strength. You, my friend, are becoming resilient to whatever life is going to throw at you next! I would only be scared or depressed if you were not growing! Now that is a dangerous place to be. And that is exactly where the enemy wants us.

The enemy wants to tell us we are not good enough, we have done nothing, we have accomplished nothing. Remind us of our failures. Remind us of our mistakes. He does that so that we stay stuck. He does this so we do not live out God's purpose for our life. But when you are experiencing pain, see that as a huge blessing! See it as a time to draw near to God and let Him take over your pain. He promises us that his yoke is easy to bear.

I always tell people this, "I am not perfect, but I'm perfecting." Let your season of difficulty be a time to perfect, learn, and grow. The game is not over my friend, it has only just begun!

So, at this point, you may be asking yourself, how do I discover my purpose?

Here is a simple equation for you:

Pain and problems = your purpose = your passion ------------> You can help others because your purpose is so meaningful to you!

So, what I am telling you is that your passion and purpose are born out of your problems and pain! Look at your moments of failure as a training ground.

What can you learn from those moments? How can your story relate to others so that you can be a blessing in other people's lives?

I am going to give you a 21-day unmasking challenge…

This is going to help you not only discover your purpose in life but also unmask yourself to share with others your story. First, I will share with you how mine began. Then I will guide you to do the same and experience the breakthrough God wants you to experience!

When I began to draw near to God and surrender my life fully to him everything began to change. This is when the mask fully fell off. When I surrendered and asked God to take over in a season of 21 days of prayer and fasting.

By day 18 specifically, I had gone through hell and had a breakthrough!

My dad's health got the worst it has ever been. I ended up in the emergency room with him twice within two weeks and the second time I thought I was going to lose him. My anxiety was heightened because of my continuous concern for his health. My relationship with my ex-partner worsened when I was most leaning into God and praying for him. He treated me with disrespect and behaved heartless towards me in the aftermath of the breakup. I felt I didn't know him anymore or maybe I never did. I continued praying for him and I was even having my sisterhood group pray for him. This heightened my anxiety because I love people and do not want anyone to harbor negativity. Around that same week, I got in a car accident and I got injured and ended up with even more problems and more anxiety from the accident and fearing my health conditions.

Everything was already in complete disarray in my life from the year of COVID. Now all this while I was praying, fasting, and leaning into God like never before! I fully surrendered to Him. I prayed to God not my will but Yours be done. How could all these bad things be happening, right?

But then the breakthrough, it looks like this...my friendships strengthened like never before. I was sharing with my sisterhood group and people close to me all that I was experiencing, and they shared with me that the wisdom and advice I was giving was a huge blessing to them. I stopped trying to go out of my way to seek forgiveness from my ex-partner for the breakup. I came to know God's tender love and forgiveness at a whole new level. Knowing God forgave me already is enough. I still pray for my ex and more than likely always will. This experience brought me to a new closeness to God that surpasses understanding. I got a new job in an industry that I am extremely passionate about. I began working on new projects such as writing my book and public speaking but this time unmasked and I began to open up to the people around me letting them know what I was going through. The beauty about being vulnerable in an imperfect world is that it makes you real. It makes you relatable. It makes you accessible in a way that enhances your ability to make an impact.

You see when you are hiding behind the mask, when you are telling everyone, you are okay when you are not, people do not learn your story. Your experiences and hardships can help others that are going through the same things as you are. Your experiences and lessons learned from them are a wealth of wisdom for others so they 1) know they are not alone and 2) they can learn from your mistakes and hopefully not make them. I hope that my story helps you to get rid of the mask.

Humility and self-awareness are essential in fulfilling your purpose. Having the humility to accept your reality and self-awareness to learn from the pain.

So here is my 21- day unmasking challenge steps for you so that you

1) Discover your purpose

2) Unmask yourself so God can use you to fulfill that purpose.

Remember this equation:

Pain & problems = your purpose = your passion

You will be passionate about your purpose because it is the pain you have experienced first-hand!

For the next 21 days you are going to pray and fast on whatever you choose. You can fast from desserts, your favorite food, social media, television or a combination of all of these. You should spend time in God's word and pray daily. Make this a priority. Don't miss a day and don't give in on your fast. Pray that God gives you His strength when you are weak. Pray for direction, vision, and clarity. Journal your thoughts and experiences daily. Finally, I recommend you write down and think about the following three questions:

What are your gifts?

What are your values?

What is your story?

Let us break these down a little. Your gifts can be anything! If your gift is talking, speak uplifting and encouraging words, give Godly advice, share wisdom. Use your gift of gab to impact others. If it is serving, then serve others. If your gift is generosity, give generously to those around you. You have a God-given gift and if you do not know what that is, ask people close to you what they see you are good at. Write a few below: (You may have one, you may have ten. This will look different for everyone and that is okay)

What do you value in life?

Do you value spending time with your family?

Having alone time to decompress?

This is important because you can be working in your gifted areas but still feel empty or unfulfilled if your values are not being met. Write your top three values below:

Finally, what is your story?

Is it a bad decision you made in life?

A miracle that happened to you?

The family environment you grew up in?

Maybe like me, your story might be a combination of these. Remember to unmask and be vulnerable. God has uniquely given you a message that is for the purpose of helping someone else's pain.

My pain had a purpose. The hardships broke me down, but they did not destroy me, and yours will not destroy you. Now that I am unmasked, I can live out my purpose to impact those around me and around the world. Now I know how to navigate life in an entirely new way I did not know how to navigate before.

Now, you, my dear friend, have learned from my pain. I hope and pray the steps I have given you will help you unmask yourself and find and fulfill your purpose. I pray you will also learn how to handle life's problems through the pain you are suffering. Remembering that it's okay to not be okay. Use the tips I have shared with you and you too will be able to impact the world and live out your purpose for the glory of God, unmasked and stronger than ever!

I cannot remind you enough that you are CHOSEN!

I must remind you because I went through a season when I did not feel chosen. I did not feel I was enough. But our feelings come and go. They ebb and flow. God's word is consistent. Today, tomorrow, and forevermore. He created you with a purpose for this moment!

Juliza Kramer is a writer, marketing and branding expert, and philanthropist. She wants to help others discover their purpose and does this by being a servant leader in her community. Serving others first has been important to her since childhood and a golden rule she still lives by today.

Her mission in life is to be the salt and light in the world and serve God daily through her gift of communication. Juliza has over 10 years' experience marketing and branding companies in South Florida where she is a native. She uses her public speaking skills to grow brands and engage and motivate professionals to discover their purpose.

Juliza embraces that everyone's story is significant to God and His people. She decided to share her story to empower business leaders, who like herself, hide behind a mask, not sharing their pain and struggles. As a businesswoman and leader, she felt she could not be vulnerable. She now sees her vulnerabilities as her biggest assets and strengths and prays that one day the business community at large will be able to do the same.

In her spare time, Juliza enjoys living an active lifestyle, reading, writing, traveling and inspiring others to find their purpose and become their most authentic self.

"Let go and let God." Is her mantra. She believes that allowing God into your problems, shortcomings and mistakes can take you to a new intimacy with God and discovering your purpose in life like never before!

To connect with Juliza you can reach her at julizakramer@gmail. com or find more information on her website coming soon. You can also find Juliza on other social media platforms such as LinkedIn, Instagram and Facebook.

STUDY 2

THE HEART TO IMPACT

You Are Chosen

"For God so loved the world that he gave his only Son, so that everyone who believes in him will not perish but have eternal life. God did not send his Son into the world to condemn it, but to save it." John 3:16-18

Recommended Readings

"Jesus said, I am the light of the world. If you follow me, you won't be stumbling through the darkness, because you will have the light that leads to life." (John 8:12)

"But the fruit of the Spirit is love, joy, peace, forbearance, kindness, goodness, faithfulness, gentleness and self-control. Against such things there is no law." (Gal. 5: 22-23)

"And so we know and rely on the love God has for us. God is love. Whoever lives in love lives in God, and God in them." (1 John 4:16)

"May the God of hope fill you with all joy and peace as you trust in him, so that you may overflow with hope by the power of the Holy Spirit." (Romans 15:13)

"Being strengthened with all power according to his glorious might so that you may have great endurance and patience." (Col. 1:11)

"Be completely humble and gentle; be patient, bearing with one another in love." (Eph. 4:2)

"I pray that out of his glorious riches he may strengthen you with power through his Spirit in your inner being, so that Christ may dwell in your hearts through faith. And I pray that you, being rooted and established in love." (Eph. 3:16-17)

Reflect - What meaning does this provide me, as His chosen one?

_____

_____

_____

_____

_____

_____

_____

_____

_____

_____

_____

_____

_____

_____

Rise Up Chosen One! -

"Get wisdom! Get understanding! Do not forget, nor turn away from the words of my mouth. Do not forsake her, and she will preserve you; Love her, and she will keep you. Wisdom is the principal thing; Therefore, get wisdom. And in all your getting, get understanding" (Proverbs 4:5-7, NKJV).

Individual Questions and Activities

Who and what defines you?

_____

_____

_____

_____

_____

_____

Action Step - Pray and ask God with a sincere heart, then wait patiently for the answer. He promised in 1 John 5:14 NET if we ask anything according to his will, he will hear us and answer us. His will is His word.

Jeremiah 29:11 says. "*For I know the plans I have for you, "Declares the Lord, "plans to prosper you and not harm you, plans to give you hope and a future*".

It is never too late to change directions. You can live above your circumstances by the choices you make. So, do not blame God when bad things happen to you. John 10:10 says, *"Satan comes to still, kill, and destroy"*. God is the one who will pull you out and protect you from evil. So, I challenge you today, to use the word of God as the yardstick by which we must live life.

Individual Activity - Define your circle of influence. In his bestselling book The 7 Habits of Highly Effective People, author Stephen R. Covey explains that truly effective people who expand their influence live a life focused on things that they can change—their circle of influence—and not things they have no power over, which can be categorized in a circle of concern.

Consider these seven (7) tips.

- Be Proactive
- Be a Active Listener
- Be Consistent
- Practice Empathy
- Accept Responsibility
- Appreciate Others
- Have a vision

Ask yourself these questions and put your answers below, as you begin the process of depicting your circles of concern and influence:

How can I leave this situation better than I found it?

_____

_____

_____

_____

_____

_____

_____

_____

_____

How can I meet and get to know new people?

_____

_____

_____

_____

_____

_____

_____

_____

How can I help and inspire the people around me?

_____

_____

_____

_____

_____

_____

_____

How can I be a solution in this situation?

_____

_____

_____

_____

_____

_____

_____

_____

Now map out your circle of concerns and influence on a separate piece of paper.

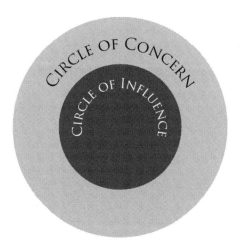

Your circle of concern is a big circle that contains everything you are worried or concerned about at the moment. Your circle of influence contains some of those things from your circle of concern because it's all the things you are worried about that you can actually change. It is the things you can influence; the problems you can do something about.

Small Group Activity:

1. Through the process of increasing self-awareness there will be people in your life that will be helpers, supporters, or distractors.

   Identify three (3) Helpers/Supporters (Inner circle of support)

   _____, _____, _____,

2. In addition to people, we also need to examine what we allow into our consciousness, look on your nightstand, in iTunes, or on your Kindle or social media posts. Are the books you're reading and the music you're listening to in alignment with your calling?

   Reflect on whether this sensory information makes you feel happier? What changes do you need to make?

   _____

   _____

   _____

   _____

   _____

   _____

   _____

   _____

3. What actions will you commit to taking in the next 30 days to live in internal alignment with your source of identity?

_____
_____
_____
_____
_____
_____
_____
_____

Small Group Discussion

Share with the group what you learned about yourself and about your circle of concerns and influence, as you pursue a heart after Christ.

Request feedback, actively listen, and integrate thoughts without providing a reaction or response. Now take a few minutes, alone, and journal how you are feeling, then take a few cleansing breaths, and write down what action you can take to reconcile others' perceptions and your own, to who God says you are.

_____
_____
_____
_____
_____

PART III

Rise Up Chosen One

A Voice At The Midnight Hour!

by Luz Rodriguez

We had just gotten evacuated on October 30, 2017, from Puerto Rico, due to the powerful Category 5 Hurricane Maria that hit and flattened the whole island. My daughter and I were evacuated from the Caribbean back to New York City. When my daughter and I arrived at JFK airport we met with my brother Juan. I was so happy to see him. I had not seen him for a while. He took our suitcases and away we went in a New York City cab. We arrived at my mother's apartment on the Lower Eastside where I was raised. We were so excited to see my mom whom I had not seen for a while either. My daughter and I resided with my mother for about two weeks, then I got a telephone call from the federal government that they had arranged for me and my daughter, Ankora Sarahi, to stay at a FEMA approved hotel. Thankfully, the hotel was located in a very quiet residential area, actually it was so close to the airport that we could see the airplanes flying over our building. However, her school was ten times as large as she was used to being in a small country school where there were only about two hundred and fifty students, and suddenly my daughter had to make new friends in a fast-paced major city and large school. Since school had already been in session a month and a half and she had to break into the crowd and make new friends, it was not hard for her to make new friends because she was a sweet girl and got along with everybody, and we were also looking forward to celebrating a festive Christmas in New York. I was so happy to be attending my home church here in New York, as it was the place where I first gave my life to Lord Jesus Christ in 1998, and I had many beautiful friends and served in the Ushering Ministry before I left for Puerto Rico. My daughter Ankora Sarahi was also dedicated to the Lord at our home church when she was just six weeks old. I named her after her two spiritual grandmothers who were very close friends of mine and that's how I got her name, so here we are. Ankora Sarah was so excited to be spending Christmas with the warm love of our family and friends.

Little did we know how dramatically and fearfully both our lives would change. I was so used to taking and picking her up from school. But the moment I started working, I had to let her go to school on her own, and she would always meet me in my workplace.

That Friday, December 21, 2018 was the last day before they went on Christmas recess, and that was the last day I saw or heard from my daughter. I remember as we both took separate trains, the last words we said to each other was "I love you."

December 21 is the shortest day of the year, but for me was the longest, darkest time of my life.

* That day I knew that I had to go out and look for her, so I left my work immediately. I got on the train. I went straight to her school, but nothing. The school building was closed. I was

walking around and around in circles where her school was. I was getting tired, hungry, the streets were getting very dark and cold. I found a bench, and I sat down and started praying and crying out to God, and that moment everything went so silent. I felt such peace in my heart, and felt such a dark situation as a mother. I started remembering and getting flashbacks of the day and night me and my daughter had to face one of the most painful storms that hit Puerto Rico on September 21, 2017. We went into our little basement, and she was sitting next to me in a chair, and I was on my knees holding her so tight and praying, and I looked at her and told her to not worry, that we were going to make it.

I took a pencil and I started writing on the wall of my basement Philippians 4:13." *I can do all things through Christ who will strengthen me*". I know that as I am sitting here on this bench to hold on tight to that same scripture again, in this dark time that I am facing where I have no answers. But even in the midst I have nowhere else to look or to go because the month of December is very cold. I had to decide whether to keep looking or go home.

So, I got up from the bench. I decided to start walking to the train station to go home, and as I was walking from the train station near my home, I decided to go to my local precinct where I live. As I opened the huge doors to the police precinct, I walked in and I went to the desk and I started explaining to the police officer who was at the desk. He then walked me to the other officer and as I sat there by this desk another officer pulled out a paper that said Missing Person's Report in capital letters. It was so impossible for me to accept that my daughter was missing.

As he finished the report, he told me that he could not file it because the policy for a missing person was 24 hours. So, I left the precinct, and I began to call on God, and began to pray and in my little hotel where my daughter and I were living. I shut the door and just began to cry to God. I was desperate so after I finished praying , I got on my cell phone and began to call all my friends to pray for my daughter, because at that moment I needed my helpers in prayers. As I called a few of my friends, I said to my best friend Nilsa, we need to make some flyers, we need to go out in the streets to find my daughter. I could not wait 24 hours until the police started to look for my daughter. You cannot tell a mother who is desperate that I had to wait 24 hours, especially when I did not even understand what was happening, when all I did was go home and cry myself to sleep every night and wonder where my daughter was, and you have no idea where to go.

I had to hold on to my faith in God. That is what was keeping me. So, from December 21, 2018, we would go outside every day looking for my daughter. I went to so many dark alleys. I had my friend Clint, drive me around mostly every day and everywhere we could go, we went looking for her. We went to housing projects; we went up the streets. Nothing at all, deep in my heart I said, I am not giving up. I will trust God because if he saw us through that rough storm I went through. AS a mother, I was not going to stop looking or giving up even though it was getting darker and darker and the more I went out in the streets, the more it got harder and harder to find her, because at the time her phone was not on, and her profile in Facebook, I could not find her.

December 25, 2018

Christmas came, her Christmas gifts were there under the Christmas tree. It was one of the hardest Christmas times I had to face without my youngest daughter. I spent Christmas by myself, hoping and waiting to see if I would hear anything from one of the detectives who was assigned to the case. Waiting in my little hotel room, listening to *O Come All Ye Faithful,* one of my favorite Christmas songs. I started to look out the window as the Christmas song was playing and suddenly tears started to shed from my eyes, and I started to say, I wonder where you are, I wonder if you are alive, I wonder if you are celebrating Christmas or even opening Christmas gifts? Where could you be? I said, oh God, please help me through this. It is very painful for me not being able to celebrate Christmas with her, and seeing her beautiful smile opening our gifts together on Christmas day, and drinking hot chocolate with lots of marshmallows and eating french toast with lots of syrup with cinnamon strawberries and bananas. It was our favorite traditional breakfast every Christmas morning.

As it was approaching midnight, I looked out the window one more time, and it was very dark and cold. All I could hear was the silence of the streets. I felt such a gentle peace in my heart, and I knew that it was the peace of God. So, I closed the window and went and laid myself to sleep because I wanted Christmas just to be over.

It was now a brand-new day and suddenly there was a hard knock at my door. When I opened the door, it was two detectives. They wanted to know more information on my daughter. But then one of them asked me for a shirt of my daughter, one that she wore a lot, so they can have one of their dogs sniff. I felt like I was in one of those T.V. crime shows like CSI New York, but it was not a show, what I was going through was real. Oh, how I wish it were just a show I was watching I said to one of the detectives. This was everyday detectives and police going to the precinct, the constant phone calls for the next couple of days after Christmas, this was my life. Did I ever think that I would be going through this now, I said to the detective, I do not understand. Why am I going through this, I do not need to understand. I am putting my hope and trust in God. I just hope my daughter is found and alive.

January 1, 2019

It was Happy New Year. But for me it was not a happy New Year. I wanted this day to really go fast like Christmas did. This day passed and nothing happened yet, it was a brand-new year and was exactly 11 days and I did not hear anything or still know the whereabouts of my daughter. Like I said the days kept getting darker and longer. I said to God, when am I going to see the light again during these hard trials I was facing. I felt like everything was so silent. But in the split of a moment my phone rings and I pick it up and a voice of one of the detectives said to me, we may have a lead on your daughter and we believe your daughter is being trafficked, I said trafficked? No way, that only happens in countries far away, not in New York City, please tell me what trafficking is, she explained to me what trafficking was, suddenly my heart dropped and at that moment I just started to cry it was like a piece of my heart was taken.

January 5, 2019

Today is the 14th day that my daughter has been missing and still has no whereabouts. It was also the first service of the New Year at my church. I decided to go to the first prayer service. As I walked into the church, I got many hugs, and we are praying for you, we are praying for Ankora Sarahi.

I knew at that moment I felt such a warm joy in my heart because it was the best place to be. As I was praying and service was almost over, I felt deep in my heart, God, has this, and I know that God is faithful. So, every time service is over, I always go somewhere to sit and have fellowship with some of my friends, especially on a Friday night. That night we went to McDonalds, which is right next to the church. I asked my three friends if we could pray. It was two brothers and my friend Juana, as we finished praying.

It was about 9:30 P.M. and my phone rang. It was the female detective, one of my favorite detectives who was incredibly involved and really helping me in finding my daughter. I heard that voice that said to me, we know who has your daughter tonight, we are going to rescue her. Wow, I started feeling excitement. She said wherever you are staying there , I will be calling you back, I said yes we are here praying.

I told her because our service just finished, before she hung up the phone she said, we need to go undercover to rescue your daughter Ankora Sarahi because she is in a dangerous situation. So, she said yes, please continue praying.

It was at that midnight hour that the detective called back to tell me we have your daughter. We rescued your daughter. It was exactly 12:01. I heard that voice at the midnight hour. My daughter was found and rescued after 14 days missing. I finally am going to see her, to see that beautiful face again. I was so overwhelmed with joy in my heart once again. God came through again, he answered my prayers, all those tears that I shedded were finally answered.

It was 2 am in the morning when a black car pulled up in front of McDonalds. I get into the car, and my friend Alan from church accompanies me to the 46th precinct. I finally got to the precinct. I was so anxious, and my eyes were full of tears. As I walked into this room there were the heroes that had found my daughter. I look over to the desk, and I see my daughter's cell phone. I said, wow, I am really going to see her. They walked me to another office, and there she was, wearing the same clothes she wore that Friday morning December 21, 2018 when she was on her way to school. I ran to her. I just started hugging and kissing her, but she looked in shock and asked me, mommy, you are not hurt, you are alive. I whispered in her ears, Ankora Sarahi. Why did you ask me? She said, mommy, the pimp that had kidnapped me told me he had hurt you and that I was not going to see you ever again. It is me and you do not know how happy I am to see you. I love you. I love you. I just started praising the Lord and thanking the detectives and police officers who were in the room. I looked over at my friend Alan who was with me, and all I could see were tears of joy falling from his eyes. After those long dark nights and gloomy days, I now get to embrace my daughter again. God turned my tears that I shed for those long 14 days of Pain, into tears of Joy.

All because of God's Faithfulness.

"I can do all things through he who strengthens me". Philippians 4:13.

My Scriptures for my daughter that I pray over her and hold dear to my heart.

"I will restore the years that the cankerworm, the palmerworm and the locust has eaten." Joel 2:25

"For I know the plans I have for you declares the Lord, plans to prosper you and not to harm you, plans to give you hope and a future". Jeremiah 29:11

Prayer Is Powerful

It is our Greatest Weapon.

God Is Faithful.

Luz Rodriguez is a Mother and a Christian Writer from New York City where she co-leads an international Christ-centered group that raises awareness and educates on Human Trafficking. This calling was put in her heart following the harrowing experience of her own daughter being kidnapped and trafficked at the age of 14. Through it all the Lord was Faithful. Luz is available for speaking engagements and workshops.

Please contact: (917) 382-4808 or
humantraffickingconnectgroup@gmail.com

THE MIRACLE
LIFE'S DISRUPTION,
THE GIFT OF LIVING

BY KANDY WINDOM

As I laid in bed, I could not feel anything, and everything was blurry. I was scared. I was dying. I have never been in this situation before. In hopes of making sense of what was happening, I looked to the left and I saw blood, people screaming and people in pain. I looked above me as I laid in the hospital bed and it was white with a bright light. I felt so confused. I looked at my mom and she was crying. I tried to talk, but there were doctors and nurses who were present and did not give me a chance to. I did not know what was happening. My legs were numb. I could not move. Suddenly…I heard a loud noise and I uttered to my mom, "I want to leave. I don't want to stay here." She ignored me and continued talking to the doctors about what was going on and then everything went dark. I had passed out.

At 18, I married the love of my life. My world revolved around him and being the best for him. We had a daughter together after a year of marriage, Nathalia. I was the happiest mother in the world. I was working hard every day, partying every weekend and all I could dream of at the time was having a house, a car and a way to go to college. I loved money and all I wanted was to be successful as a wife, mother and hard worker.

119

I wore the best and most expensive dresses. I loved getting the attention from men so that women would hate it and then did not want to be around me. Everything was perfect. I had a home and an amazing family until one afternoon, I received a message from my coworker that my husband was seeing another woman. I entered into panic and my whole world completely ended in that moment. I felt lost. We decided to go our separate ways.

After a year, my husband was talking to me very nicely again since I lost weight and I was more attractive to him. I even invited him to go out and I paid for everything that night. It was one of the most incredible moments we had as a couple again. I got drunk, he got drunk, and we had sex. Being that we had alcohol in our systems, I didn't even remember that it happened, but it felt like everything was so perfect again. I got home super happy that night. Maybe because of the drinks.

At 24 years old, I was happy, and I felt like everything was working out in my favor again. We ended up talking for a few weeks on the phone. He was so sweet that I fell in love again before I noticed that I did not get my cycle. Was I pregnant? I did not know what else to think so I jumped up from where I was sitting and walked straight to the public phone to call him. My heart was so happy because I was going to give him this huge news. I knew we were separated, but I was so sure that things would work out, so I finally called him and shared the news. Sadly, he replied to me saying, "This is not mine. You have been going out with another guy. Don't you think it may be his?" At that moment, I felt like I got shot in the heart. My throat closed, I could not breathe, and I felt tremendous pain all over my body.

I felt like I was going to pass out before I told him, "It's okay. Don't worry about it," and hung up the phone. That was the last time I talked to him for months.

Four months later, I was let go from my job because I was pregnant. I did not have any money and I was rejected for many job applications due to being pregnant. I also moved to my parents' house since I did not have any money, a job, or a husband to support me. My belly was growing and growing. I felt sick most of the time and I could not believe I was back to living with my parents at age 24. It was devastating and I felt like a failure for being rejected by my husband. I felt old. What man would love me with two kids?

I remember sitting outside the house and I thought, "Wow...all those dresses, parties and nice things that I had are all gone." I had a great job in an office for an HR department. I was taking classes at the college, but now I did not have money. I had to quit school. I could not even afford to pay for a bus ride anymore. I realized I did not have a purpose for my life anymore. At that very moment outside my house, I touched my belly and I said to my baby, 'Everything will be okay," even though I did not believe what I said.

A few months passed and the moment came. Still having no money in my wallet or support from my husband, I was getting ready to have my baby. My mom ran to the phone to call him and I was rejected once again by my husband. I did not have any money and I was unsure if I would be able to pay or get medicine in the community I was in. I was right. No pain medicine unless you had the money to pay for the delivery of my child. I remember that it was raining very hard that day. I had so much pain and I didn't even have acetaminophen while in the hospital because of not having any sort of income or help with money. The next thing I know, I was in labor and they told me to push extremely hard. I cried because the pain was so strong; a pain I have never felt before. I did not feel my legs, my heart was fast, and I was sweating. The nurse manipulated my body to help me push and the doctor cut me without any pain medication. I could not believe I was going through all this alone. My mother was there, but the father of my child was not. I stayed in a hospital and I was treated like an animal.

After everything that I went through, it did not matter because I had just brought life into the world, my son Alejandro. When I saw him, I felt immense joy, but not long after, I had a seizure. The hospital discharged me a day later still in excruciating pain, but I was so grateful to have my baby with me. My son's father never called and never came to see us. No one knew it, but I felt like I was dying.

Thankfully and out of nowhere, an older gentleman who was a good Samaritan bought everything for my son from diapers to food and anything else we needed. He brought me chicken and eggs every week.

Two weeks had passed before my husband finally came to talk to me. I was feeding my newborn baby at the time and he was 15 days old. Turns out that my husband was relocating to Spain the next day and if I wanted to register our son under his name, he was giving me his permission since we were still married. Then he said goodbye to our daughter and left. All of this happened in March 2000. At the time, I decided to go live with my sister, and I started having a lot of problems with my breathing because I was so overweight. I do not remember how much I was weighing, but man I was huge. I cried every night while my babies were sleeping. I could not even breathe during the night, so I had to sleep in an upright seated position. At least my baby was healthy and so beautiful, which made it all worth it.

There was a silver lining even in this painful experience. My little sister got engaged and her wedding was set for May 10th. I was so excited and happy to see my sister happy. This meant I would be going to the beauty salon to get my hair done with a good friend. My sister and I are close and even though things were not well in my life, it was amazing to witness her joy and to dream that it could be mine again one day.

Then I had a disruption yet again. With my baby in my arms, I noticed that he was feeling cold or so I thought. When I looked at him, he started shaking uncontrollably. I did not understand what was happening. I was confused. Then, I realized he was having a seizure. I could not move as I was in shock and I could not even talk or make any movements. My friend grabbed my hand and pulled me over to run to the medical center. We ran as fast as we could while my son kept having a seizure again and again. I was crying at the medical center and then we were transported to a children's hospital. My baby was only 3 months old when he got diagnosed with Meningitis. When your kids are in danger, pain or distress, you forget about yourself and the world seems to stop. You cannot breathe.

This time, I stayed with my baby in the hospital for a month. I was sleeping every night in a plastic chair and I took baths in a church next to the hospital. The nuns offered me food every day. Everyone who saw my son fell in love with him. I received free clothes for him, and the nuns paid some money for the time he was in the hospital. My daughter was healthy and at home. Thank God her grandmother was taking care of her so that I could focus on my son. When my son was discharged from the hospital, I started to breathe again. My life was restored.

This was in June 2000, I was 25 years old, and all my family was happy to see my son getting better although we did not know if he was going to have speech problems or if he was going to be able to walk at the time. A few days passed and then I noticed my body was still swelling and getting fat. Every time I walked, I had to stop and take a breath. My clothes were getting too tight. Again, I found myself with no money, no job, no husband and no insurance so my mom advised me to tell my grandpa, Oscar. He helped me gain access to a doctor who could refer me to a clinic. I got there and the doctor asked to take my clothes off, which I thought was weird, but I did it. He then examined me and took my blood pressure. The doctor told my mom to take me to urgent care immediately, so I asked him why and he said there was a need to find out what was happening to me internally. He asked if I had insurance and I did not, but my grandpa offered to pay for the medical care. I got to the clinic and they put me on an IV and gave me some food. I spent the night there because my blood pressure was exceedingly high. I honestly did not feel anything. The only thing I could feel is that I could not breathe. When my doctor came in the next morning, he looked up so nervous and asked me how I was feeling. I told him that I was tired and that I could not breathe. I felt my chest getting tight. My mom saw me, she told me my face looked huge. I did not understand and then all the equipment started beeping. The doctor was having a conversation with my mom, but not loud enough to where I could hear what they were saying. Then everything went dark, but I was still trying to listen.

I was told later that I was transported by ambulance to a hospital, as I needed a higher level of care (oxygen and equipment not available at the clinic). When I became conscious, I could not understand what was happening, then I passed out again, and everything went dark.

I was pushed by two nurses to the 4th floor. I kept asking my mom, "Am I going to die?" She kept saying, "everything is going to be okay." As I arrived on the 4th floor, I was between two young ladies, one had Hepatitis and the other one had HIV. We did not have dividers or curtains. The room was cold and there were 12 patients on that floor. I looked around and I felt like nothing. I thought to myself, "This is it. It is my time." Then, surprisingly I saw my grandfather who was 70 years old walking towards me, and he looked to the nurses and told them, "What are you giving her?" My grandfather monitored all the meds they were giving me and made me drink Gatorade when the doctors and nurses were not looking. He spent all 33 nights with me sleeping on the floor and making sure I was treated well. The old ladies were so surprised to see me there. They told me, "You are so young to be here." Those ladies made me think and I thought about my past experiences, my decisions, what I had done and what I had not done. 3 days later, a lady died next to me and two older ladies died from heart attacks. I asked my grandpa to take me to the bathroom. I could not even walk, but I pushed myself to do it. I got there and I looked at myself in the mirror. I started having a conversation to myself. I said, "Kandy, you are just 25 years old, what do you want? Where do you want to go? You have 2 beautiful kids who need your support. What are you doing here?" I kept saying these questions over and over and I could not find the answers. I did not see light in my eyes. There was only sadness. I knew I was under so many medications, monitors, IVs, etc....so I asked my grandfather to take me back to bed. While I was walking, he told me that my dad won a lottery and that I have all the meds needed to feel better and that I will not die. I looked at his eyes and started crying and I hugged my grandpa. Man, I did not cry for two weeks. I was holding those emotions that were killing me inside. I took my first step towards recovery and I said, "I am not dying. This will pass. I am strong. I can do this. Everything I need is within me. God is with me." I felt God was there and I began feeling that I was walking over the air in slow motion. I saw every step slowly. Those were the longest 13 steps in my life. It was my 12th day in the hospital, on the floor where patients were dying. The nurses did not have hope for me, but my grandpa, parents and God did have hope for me. On day 21, I did not feel like the same person I was before my heart failure. I felt reborn! This was an awakening experience. I asked my grandpa and my mom to bring me music and on the 25th day, they moved me to a private room until I left the hospital.

When I looked outside, it felt different. I noticed the mountains, the trees, the breeze and my mom's perfume. I smiled and I thanked God, my grandpa and my parents for what they did to me. I felt so grateful, but also angry because I let myself go and gave permission for others to control my life. "Enough is enough," I yelled to myself and I decided it was time for a new life. For a new me! In this experience, I learned that everything happens for a reason. There was a reason why my son got sick, a reason for my husband to cheat on me and abandon my family, and a reason for me to experience death. I was not grateful for what I had before. I thought I deserved it. I was living life in turn with my husband instead of myself. I thought he was the only man out there for me and that if he did not love me, I was not meant to be loved. I remember when I asked my husband for a divorce, I told him, "Give me permission to take my kids and leave the country because I am leaving, and you won't get the opportunity to see your kids ever again. I am going to be married and I will be so happy." I did not know it was going to be true. I thought it was a huge lie, but I yelled at him from my heart that he will not see us again and guess what, he did not. I remarried 6 months later, and I came to the United States and settled in California when I was 26 years old. At the time, my son Alejandro was 1 year old, and Nathalia was 6 years old. This is the power of words. I learned to be careful about what I say, but I am so happy I did. During this experience, I learned 3 things: to live now, to lead from my heart, and to never give up.

- Everything starts with your deepest self and living the present moment.

Do you know how many times you lived in the wrong time? I was living in the wrong time, the sad past and the uncertain future. In my mind, there was only negative talk. Nobody will love a woman with two kids, I do not have money, so I will not have friends and so on. I had to leave everything including furniture and clothes back in Colombia when I came to California. I arrived in the United States with just my kids and was ready to see what was next in my life. I did not know that my new husband had the opportunity to give me everything. Thinking now, when I met him, he won my heart just by the way he looked at my kids with love and that was the only thing I cared about. I was hungry for love and happiness. That is why I said yes to him. My husband gave me everything I needed to feel better. I was taking 21 medications a day for my heart, now I only take 1 pill a day. This amazing man put me with the best doctors, and he did not care if I worked or not. He only wanted me to go to school, learn English and take care of the house so I did. I have been living day by day since then.

I learned that everything starts with your deepest self and living in the moment. I enjoyed my walks with my kids, the play time, the movie time and the wine nights with my husband. Serving my husband and being a good wife has always been what I wanted. When I was in my 20's, I was almost snatched by human traffickers because I was so eager to have money and material stuff that I almost put myself in dangerous situations.

Even if it is a glass of water that you only are having today, say thank you to God and the Universe or whoever you believe in. I did not say thank you and I do not even remember the good things that happened to me. I was only focused on the negative things. Now that I say thank you, I meditate and I live in the now, I receive so many blessings. I have a huge house the way I dreamt of, but I never asked. I have money and I do not ask for that either. Money comes without even asking. Now it is time to become a better version of yourself. Enjoy the present moments.

- Leading within you from your heart

My life was so superficial. My vocabulary was, "I want this, and I want that." The feelings are not the same anymore. The outcomes are completely different. While I was focused on the outside, I lost myself inside. I was depending on someone's love to feel love and I was depending on acceptance from others to feel secure. I learned during this experience that love means to love myself first. By that I mean, growing spiritually, knowing my standards and boundaries, self-awareness, self-management, relationship management, and looking at myself in the mirror with confidence and love. It is loving everything about myself and growing every day because I am the creation of God. My life was led by two needs: security and certainty. That is why I was in pain, experienced suffering and felt stuck. The moment that I decided to do an auto evaluation of myself to know my weakness, strength, opportunities and threads (SWOT Analysis), I started focusing on my strength and opportunities. I learned that I only have control of what I do, my actions. I remembered my cardiologist told me back in Colombia, "If you want to live and see your grandchildren, you must change." Check this out...he did not say I should change. He said I MUST change. I did not understand why he said that and what I needed to do, but now

I understood that I do not need to live the same way and that is what I did. I began to say yes to life, yes to change and yes to new opportunities. I do not live a life driven by my ego anymore. I lead and live my life from my heart. One way that helped me was meditation. It took me years to learn and be consistent, but it was well worth it.

I also joined the John Maxwell Team to learn more leadership skills that I could develop. You cannot find all your answers from your experiences; however, you can learn from others' experiences and that is why I joined the team. "Leadership is influence. Nothing more, nothing less," says John Maxwell. How much influence do you have in yourself? Can you control everything? These questions just made me think of this incredible movie called Inside Out. During the movie, all the emotions worked hard to avoid sadness, to take control and in the movie they all learned that it needed to happen to have joy. Happiness is defined as an experience of joy, contentment or positive well-being. It is when life is good, meaningful and worthwhile. You can see that joy is super important and you want to be there and have a meaningful life, but you also need those negative emotions to find balance. Do not feel discouraged if you are feeling sad now or angry.

I remember that I made the most important decision of my life when I was angry. The most important thing is how fast you can turn that emotion around when it happens. That is why leading from your heart and influencing yourself to find your happiness is important.

- Empowering Beliefs and Yes Strategy

There were so many situations that made my heart fail, but something I am sure about is that I never give up and I have faith. My family supported me all the way without questions. Now, you must understand that change is a transformation, and that transformation happens when there is something you need to let go. There is a bridge between who your old self is and who you are now. If someone succeeds during that transformation, the difference is in how you react and what actions you take. I made the decision to live. I did not have a clear idea of how I was going to do it. I let God show me the path and had faith in every step in this process. I know it was painful for me and you may be going through a painful situation too. Please do not give up on living. Do you know how many people have paid millions of dollars trying to find a cure, so we do not die? The secret is to choose to live and never give up on your life. Words have power and you have the power to choose your destination. You have been chosen to do something greater in this life. Whatever happened yesterday, it was yesterday. You should not be carrying this heavy luggage for the rest of your life. Let that go. Put the luggage down and start living the life you always wanted now. There are situations in life that are going to be very painful, but there are also situations that will be a blessing to you. Which one would you pick? Remember, whatever you focus on will expand so choose wisely.

For many years I complicated my life by focusing on material things instead on what is most important for me and my family. Now I travel around the world, I finished my master's in human resources and so many certifications and licenses. I opened my own coaching and training practice. I have a successful and loving family and my kids are super smart and love giving to others. All these would not be possible if I did not have the courage to change, to risk, to sacrifice and to love myself enough to raise my standards and change my needs. Now my primary needs are to love and give. All I want is to make a better world and that is possible if I touch one person at the time, starting with you. You are worth it. You are a unique human being that has a huge purpose in this life and God will show you the path. You must trust the journey and enjoy every step in this process.

Kandy Windom, born in Cali, Colombia, is a mother of three, family oriented, a traveler and a huge believer of living NOW. Kandy is the CEO and founder of KW Coaching Group, an Executive Director of the John Maxwell Team, and a graduate from Webster University with a Master's in Human Resources. She is also a facilitator, speaker, and trainer, with an expertise in talent development for over a decade. Twenty years ago, Kandy had a transformational event that changed her life forever. With her passion for growing and celebrating life, Kandy shares her wisdom through her coaching and training programs that have influenced and touched many people around the world.

Kandy Windom, MA
KW Coaching Group
400 North Tampa Street, 15th Floor
Tampa, FL 33602
813.304.8946
support@kandywindom.com

www.kandywindom.com
Social Media Links
https://www.linkedin.com/in/kwindom/
https://www.facebook.com/KandyNWindom

WALKING INTO LOVE, FINDING MY TRUE KING.......

BY ALEJANDRA VICENT

This chapter is a little different, as I want to share something that as a teenager, I feel we all go through. And that is why my title is called walking into love and not falling in love.

Sometimes as a little one we are called a princess. Through Disney movies, friends, and society in general. We are told that we will find a prince, fall in love, have a castle, and live happily ever after. That is the fairy tale that every young person wishes they could have.

As I think to myself, we all know it generally does not go that way. (Spoiler alert, we all know that stories can end differently)

Going through my early relationships, I wanted the fairytale story that meant feeling respected, protected, loved, and heard, but due to all the things that were happening such as miserably failed first love, domestic violence, and cheating. Chasing the fairytale became my priority.

Being a human being and being a woman, we all know that curiosity occurs when we start to have feelings. I was never taught the importance of having boundaries or even knew what codependency was. I was taught to respect others, but never taught to respect myself. Like many young people, even coming from the best family most of the time this is not something we learn other than with life experience and lots of work. I felt insecurities which led me to people-pleasing. Consequently, I walked into relationships unprepared and setting myself up for failure.

As a 40-year-old woman with the knowledge that comes with experience, I want to share a story that changed my life and that I am hoping will change yours.

A little over a year ago, I met a man who is totally different than what I am used to. I remember that day like it was yesterday. My cousin came to Florida from North Carolina to visit me for the weekend. I had been going through an emotional rollercoaster since my divorce, from a marriage of almost 10 years. My cousin and I have always connected on many levels, especially communication, life experiences, and of course sister's love. I was filled with anticipation and excitement knowing that she was coming to visit me. We have so much in common, including our feelings of just going with the flow.

She arrived on a Friday about 9am and she waited for me to pick her up at the airport. I must mention that I picked her up around 10:30am, since I fell asleep. Our plans were to spend time together no matter what or where because we both knew when we're together, we made the best out of anything. I had to work that day, so I decided to take her with me. I am not sure she knew that, but I knew she would be okay with it. After putting her to work on her vacation, we decided to get something to eat and then go home and prepare ourselves for a night out into town.

Our meal turned into a two hour long affair. So, I suggested we just go to the mall instead, since it was very close to us. We could buy some high heels and just pretend we were all dressed up. She agreed with me, so we went to the mall to get our shoes. We ended up buying boots instead that were not dressy at all, but we were having fun and I really fell in love with those boots. At that moment, she made a suggestion that ultimately changed my life. She said to me, "how about we go to the Hard Rock Casino, since I haven't been there since the renovation?" I am always up for a good time so we went.

We walked around as we caught up on life. We went to the bar to get a drink and while the bartender made it, we started to have a conversation with a lady sitting next to us. To make a long story short, she introduced us to her husband, who at the same time, also introduced us to his friends. About 20 minutes later, another group of their friends came, including the man that has changed my life, Brad Cohen.

He shook my hand as he said, "Wow, I like your handshake," soon after meeting each other. Brad suggested we all go to a high limit lounge to get a bite to eat. We all decided to go, but right before walking into the place Brad and I started a conversation. I must say that I was attracted to him, but even more so after talking to him for four hours by the end of that night.

You might be asking what about my cousin? She was also having a great time, gambling and chatting with the rest of the people. Right before meeting Brad, I had exchanged numbers with Michelle, who was part of the couple that introduced us to everyone. So, Brad and I somehow did not exchange our numbers that night. However, I knew I could find him through Michelle if I really wanted to. Sure enough, the next day I received a text message from Michelle asking if Brad could have my number and I said yes. Brad and I started texting each other over the course of several days, getting to know each other a little bit more each day. Through this time, I continue with my daily routine working as a manager in a restaurant, doing some of my life coaching and being a mom.

Soon Brad invited me to lunch, and I was excited to see him. We had a nice time at our lunch as we shared a little bit of everything. We continued our chats via text learning more about each other with each passing day and for those of you with wandering minds, know we did not kiss yet!

I remember about a month after meeting each other. I was at work and I texted him saying, "Brad, how about you drive to my job and text me when you are outside?". I'll get in your car and we'll kiss without saying a word." He agreed and I waited patiently for his text that would announce his arrival. 30 minutes later he texted me. I walked out, I got in his car and we kissed. We both smiled after kissing and I went back to work thinking, "Oh my God, this man really knows how to kiss! His lips are delicious."

We continued seeing and learning about each other. He was committed and patient. Not rushing through the process and letting the pieces fall into place like building a puzzle. As I said before, he was totally a different man unlike any other man I have ever encountered and beyond comparison.

Brad is 52 years old and full of energy. A man with a head on his shoulders. He is self-made, owning multiple successful businesses, which he and his family have built from the ground up. Brad is also driven by his physical condition, working out five days a week, an hour and a half at a time. He is also an amazing father of three beautiful young adults. In short, Brad is a complete man.

Although we come from totally different backgrounds, both culturally and religiously. We respect and admire each other's differences. We always have fascinating conversations. That being said, Brad would ask me so many questions. He would ask me about my childhood, my future, everything and anything he thought up. I must say it was uncomfortable at first, considering I always thought of myself as a talker, I was never asked so many specific questions. We continued to spend hours of amazing quality time together, such as eating at restaurants, trips, cooking and just enjoying each other. Realizing with each passing day that we had so much in common and I thought it was crazy how we clicked so well. However, the toughness and directness of his questions created an uncomfortable situation. Amazingly so, being uncomfortable was exactly what I needed because it allowed us to get to a much more intimate place emotionally. Suddenly, COVID-19 hits, and I was not able to work. We got to spend even more time together including sleepovers that turned into, pretty much, us living together. We just enjoyed being with each other so much, in a sense the virus worked in our favor.

My childhood was full of confusions, full of instabilities, and full of many things that created a lot of insecurities for me as an adult. Some things we do not realize will affect us later in life. I have an amazing family, but with varying degrees of dysfunctionality, as with many families. I will be more specific on this in a future chapter.

As we started our relationship and have become more comfortable with each other, Brad had shared with me how he has been working on himself with a therapist for the last 6 years. I loved to learn that about him, since I am a life coach, so our conversations are always very deep. I have also done a lot of work on myself surrounding anxiety, depression and panic attacks for the last 10 years. You can read more of that in a previous book, for which I wrote a chapter.

I mentioned to Brad that I would like to do a session together with his therapist since I love the growth. Boy oh boy, was this a mind trip! Never in a million years I would have thought that with one therapy session, I was going to discover so much about myself. The reasons for many of my actions and reactions to events throughout my life and the realization of how much our childhood experiences impact us as adults. Seeing how beneficial this was for me, we agreed to continue going together to therapy. I especially loved doing the work with a support team and having such an amazing man by my side. I have also come to understand that I was a people-pleaser, I have never created any boundaries with anyone, and that I also had a lot of patterns that needed to change.

The personal growth was so amazing, that I also incorporated therapy sessions just for me by my lonesome. In a short time, I realized that I did not know who I was as a person. Getting to know myself has allowed me to realize that by switching some things around, I can completely be the woman I always wanted to be. It has brought a new sense of purpose and direction to my life. You should also know that this process has not been a cakewalk either, doing the work has not been easy. Especially, when you must revisit painful childhood memories I had already stored, locked and thrown away the key never to resurrect them again. Nevertheless, seeing that it is all necessary I am willing to do whatever it takes. Yes, I am a type A personality. Meaning I am competitive, ambitious, and yes, I am also impatient. So, add these ingredients into my head recipe and all I said to myself was "Lady, you better strap on your seatbelt; it's going to be a bumpy ride."

Having Brad there to support me through it all, has been mind-blowing to say the least. For the first time in my life, I felt liberated to open up to Brad about so many things from my past. Frankly, I should have a hunchback from the heavy load I have been carrying all these years. I have always been closed off with everyone about my childhood. I created a wall where I have never allowed anyone in other than my God.

Thanks to my relationship with Jesus Christ and my faith in my creator, I have always felt protected, loved and understood.

Consequently, I never saw a need to let anyone else see deep inside of me, because with my lord by my side I knew everything would be okay.

Today, I sit here knowing the real meaning of respect, relationship, open communication, making love, and most of all truly knowing who I am. I now have new goals and I am free to choose my own path. The road ahead looks promising armed with my superhero utility belt. Full of all the tools I need to be in a healthy, loving, caring relationship with my two beautiful daughters, my family and friends, and with the most amazing man that God has created, Brad Cohen.

Brad and I have been together for a little over a year now. We have done an extreme amount of therapeutic work as a couple during that time. This therapeutic work represents; in my opinion; three years' worth of progress in a relationship. This is without including how we have been going deep into our deepest secrets. That has given us the freedom as individuals and the power of trust as a couple. Today, I can openly say that Brad knows me more than anyone has in my entire life. We know and understand each other without even saying a word.

By this point in the chapter, you may be asking, "How do I reach this level of intimacy in my relationship?" First, it does not just happen by itself. It takes a lot of work and perseverance. Second, it takes a willingness to feel uncomfortable, and some courage to power through those uncomfortable moments and times.

I have found that many relationships come with a heavy dose of codependency. I find that particularly true when the man is of a strong personality. That is why one of the goals with this chapter is that every person learns the importance of appropriate boundaries, routines, therapies by getting to know yourself as a person. With these we can have healthy relationships and, if we have them, raise our kids to be mentally ready to face the world. I know they have choices and decisions that are much different than those I faced, and they face them every day.

Reaching significant levels of intimacy in a relationship is awesome, now how do I maintain it? Work and more work, but it is worth every bit of it.

Both Brad and I continue to see our therapists, both individually and together. Brad helped me to understand that seeing a therapist when things are good helps us to avoid some pitfalls and work our way through others more easily and to not only see one when there is a problem. It also helps maintain the intimacy, because we are both transparent when we do it as a couple.

I also do a lot of work on my own, through reading, learning how to better communicate, so that we do not create situations where we hear different things that our partner has said. It is through active listening that I hear everything Brad says and respond appropriately.

One of the best methods of maintaining intimacy with Brad comes from some of our rituals. For example, we pray and meditate daily, together. It helps to know what is important for each of us and has a tendency to temper any issues that we might be having between us.

Another ritual that is important to us is knowing that one night a week is just for the two of us. For us it is Wednesday nights. Brad and I go out alone every Wednesday night. It might just be to dinner, or the casino. But we both know that we are going to have each other's sole attention for one night per week.

Although we have several other times when quality times exist for us, Wednesday nights are a given and we both look forward to it.

Finally, and perhaps most importantly, respect and patience. It is important that I know that even when we disagree, I am going to be treated with respect every time and he knows the same. Knowing that helps us both to keep a level of patience that gets us through every problem.

As for me, thank you Lord, for giving me the gift of a man that has opened the doors for me to grow so I can be happy, respected and loved, that is what a true king does.

Love,

Your breath of fresh air, Your true queen.

Alejandra "Allie" Vicent is a life coach living and working in South Florida.

She is getting her Life Coach Diploma at the University of Miami. As she has years of experience with life coaching, she is also a volunteer in many nonprofit organizations where she helps raise money and coach others.

A life coach is a type of wellness professional who helps people make progress in their lives in order to attain greater fulfillment. Life coaches aid their clients in improving their relationships, careers, and day-to-day lives. Life coaches can help you clarify your goals, identify the obstacles holding you back, and then come up with strategies for overcoming each obstacle. In creating these strategies, life coaches target your unique skills and gifts. By helping you to make the most of your strengths, life coaches provide the support you need to achieve long-lasting change.

Allies mission is to help people to take the steps necessary to overcome any circumstance. She is consistently working on new ideas to assist her clients and move them forward.

After a few failed relationships throughout her life, Allie realized God had her soul mate waiting for her all along. She's joyfully coupled with her dream-come-true life partner who completes her. She has two beautiful daughters, aged 19 and 9 and they are the absolute gift of her life.

Allie has found that many relationships come with a heavy dose of codependency. Her goal in writing is that every person learns the importance of appropriate boundaries, routines, therapies by getting to know themself more.

954-729-7238
Facing Anxiety with Allie
facinganxietywithallie@gmail.com

STUDY 3

RISE UP CHOSEN ONE

She is an image-bearer. (Genesis 1:27, NIV) God created the woman to be a strong ally—a warrior. (Eph. 6:10-11). The description of Lady Wisdom personified as a woman in Proverbs 31 is full of battle words—like valor, strength, and prey. Woman is a co-regent and co-heir. Woman is a force to be reckoned with on the battlefield of life.

"We are fearfully and wonderfully made." (Psalm 139:14)

Recommended Readings

"A gracious woman attains honor," (Proverbs 11:16)

"The wise woman builds her house, But the foolish tears it down with her own hands." (Proverbs 14:1)

"And looking at them Jesus said to them, "With people this is impossible, but with God all things are possible." (Mathew 19:26)

"Strength and dignity are her clothing, And she smiles at the future." (Proverbs 31:25)

"Now, my daughter, do not fear. I will do for you whatever you ask, for all my people in the city know that you are a woman of excellence." (Ruth 11:3)

Our shared and primary purpose is to become disciples (followers) of Jesus Christ. Our secondary callings are unique and are birthed out of our submission to the primary calling. To practice this truth, we must understand God's loving message toward all women.

To all God's daughters everywhere: We have a responsibility to remember our identity in Christ and the work of the Lord in our lives. Since we are all created in the image of God, we must compassionately embrace God's message for all women.

Reflect - What meaning does this provide me, as His chosen one?

_____

_____

_____

_____

_____

_____

_____

_____

_____

_____

_____

_____

Rise Up Chosen One! -

"Get wisdom! Get understanding! Do not forget, nor turn away from the words of my mouth. Do not forsake her, and she will preserve you; Love her, and she will keep you. Wisdom is the principal thing; Therefore, get wisdom. And in all your getting, get understanding" (Proverbs 4:5-7, NKJV).

Individual Questions and Activities

1. As women we are tasked to wear many different hats in different stages of life. We remain the primary caregiver in our households, whether it be to our parents, our children, or others in need. We were created as - The Helper [The term also has the meaning of someone who brings another to fulfillment, Exodus 18:4; Deuteronomy 33:7; Psalms 10:14; 33:20].

   Now more than ever, we are a significant part of the financial stability of our households, and with increasing incidents, we are assuming leadership roles in all fields.

   In some ways our secondary and tertiary callings are defined by our circumstances. But we were created and equipped to rise above circumstances and be His light bearer in all circumstances.

To the single women: Your singleness is a gift from the Lord, even when it doesn't feel that way. Be generous with your gifts, and treasure the time God has given you to worship him without distraction.

To the wives: God doesn't just want to change your husband to give him a hope and a future. God wants to transform you as well. Look up in reverence to God. Watch and pray.

To the widows: God understands you have suffered an extreme loss. Take time to grieve and care for your soul, and understand that your loss is not the end of the journey. God still has a purpose for you, and he will comfort you and give you peace.

To the single mothers: God sees you! Like Hagar lost in the desert with a crying baby and no resources, God will provide for you and your children. Trust him and obey.

To the barren women: Throughout the Bible, God used countless faithful women—like Miriam, the prophetess Huldah, Mary of Bethany, Priscilla—and we don't know if they ever had children.

To the mothers: You are not in charge of your children's salvation. God is. After a certain point in life, you are not even responsible for their choices. They are. Model for them a life devoted to God, train them, and release them to God's care.

To the women who work outside the home: Like Deborah and the model of the Proverbs 31 woman, God has enlarged your territory. Do not take your opportunities to influence lightly. Glorify God in your work.

To the older women: There is no such thing as "retiring" from God's kingdom work. Run your race faithfully until the end. Walk, roll, or limp if necessary, but don't give up on the journey!

Remain faithful and diligent. Take women under your wings and be an example of how to finish well!

To the younger women: Respect your elders. Sit at their feet and learn from them. There is nothing new under the sun (Ecclesiastes 1:9). [Exerb by Natasha Sistrunk Robinson]

1. In this season of your life how can you balance your passion(s) with the demands of life, work, and calling?

_____

_____

_____

_____

_____

_____

_____

_____

_____

_____

_____

_____

_____

_____

_____

_____

_____

2. If you have an identified calling but haven't acted upon it, reflect on the reason(s) why and write them down. What blocks are preventing you from living it out?

_____

_____

_____

_____

_____

_____

_____

_____

3. What are 3-5 actions you can take in the next 30 days to eliminate some of the blocks?

_____

_____

_____

_____

_____

_____

_____

_____

_____

_____

_____

4. What are you currently waiting for? Pray on some activities that will prepare you to receive what you're waiting for and write them down.

_____

_____

_____

_____

_____

_____

_____

_____

5. Reflect on the story you wrote in the first section of Chosen. What else needs to be added to your Chose Workbook now?

_____

_____

_____

_____

_____

_____

_____

_____

_____

6. What lessons can someone learn from your story?

_____
_____
_____
_____
_____
_____
_____
_____
_____

7. Why is that important to you?

_____
_____
_____
_____
_____
_____
_____
_____
_____
_____
_____
_____
_____
_____
_____

8. Make an action plan for the next 30 days on a separate piece of paper. Write here how you will take action on what you've learned from Chosen? Compile all of the Action Steps you will take into one master list, then prioritize the list (with first being the most urgent), assign dates and get them on your calendar!

    _____

    _____

    _____

    _____

    _____

    _____

    _____

    _____

    _____

9. Set your vision goal. Where do you want to be on this date, three years from now?

    _____

    _____

    _____

    _____

    _____

    _____

    _____

    _____

    _____

<u>Action Step</u> - Pray and ask God with a sincere heart, then wait patiently for the answer. He promised in 1 John 5:14 NET if we ask anything according to his will, he will hear us and answer us. His will is his word.

Jeremiah 29:11 says. *"For I know the plans I have for you, "Declares the Lord, "plans to prosper you and not harm you, plans to give you hope and a future".*

It is never too late to change directions. You can live above your circumstances by the choices you make. So, do not blame God when bad things happen to you. John 10:10 says, *"Satan comes to still, kill, and destroy".* God is the one who will pull you out and protect you from evil. So, I challenge you today, to use the word of God as the yardstick by which we must live life.

<u>Small Group Activity</u> - Consider

We must treat every person, male and female, with dignity because they bear God's image and are precious to him.

We must treat others as we would want to be treated—the second Great Commandment. In fact, we are told to treat them as if they were Christ: "I was hungry and you fed me…naked and you clothed me…."

We must treat people with respect for their God-given dignity at every stage of life. The *imago Dei* is why so many Christians are pro-life—because every life, even unborn life, is made in the image of God. But sometimes we fail to see the ramifications of the *imago Dei* at other stages of life…how we handle domestic violence, homelessness, poverty, bullying, human trafficking, sexual abuse, euthanasia, and so much more.

We must stop teaching stereotypes as if they are based in scripture. Jacob cooked stew. Jesus cooked fish. The male deacons—not the women's ministry—served food to the Greek widows. Paul let himself be beat up in Philippi, and Jesus allowed himself to be stripped and spit on—great insults to manhood. Mary of Bethany sat in the traditional pose of a male seminary student as she studied Torah at Jesus's feet—and Jesus told the woman who expected her to stay in the kitchen to back off. All these and more suggest that we must always rank following Christ and spiritual priorities higher that conforming to cultural gender norms—even if that culture is the Christian bubble.

We must seek to create male/female partnerships instead of segregating everything. Some see involvement of women as a man-fail, but male-and-female partnerships are essential to "subduing the earth" and *imago-Dei*-ing together. Does your women's ministry seek male input on the studies you choose? Do all the committees at your church have both men and women providing input? When you invite people to come to the front of the sanctuary for prayer, do you make sure you have both men and women ready to welcome them? (Imagine if a sexually abused woman fears men. Seeing a female to whom she can talk knocks down an unnecessary barrier.)

In a world in which #MeToo and #ChurchToo remind us that brokenness has infiltrated every part of society including the church, the Bible's truths are absolutely relevant. When God brought *ishah* (woman) to *ish* (man), he called their partnership "very good." Let us show by our words and actions that we believe his words to be true.

Small Group Discussion

Share with the group how you proactively get involved in your community or with others, to promote collaboration, while cultivating within yourself, a heart after Christ.

Request feedback, actively listen, and integrate thoughts without providing a reaction or response. Now take a few minutes, alone, and journal how you are feeling, then take a few cleansing breaths, and write down what action you can take to reconcile others' perceptions and your own, to who God says you are.

_____

_____

_____

_____

_____

_____

_____

_____

_____

_____

_____

NOTE OF APPRECIATION

The saying, "It takes a village" could not be a more accurate description of Elite Foundation's operant philosophy. The Foundation is a 501(c)(3) nonprofit organization that stands in the gap to educate, empower and to help others evolve into their full potential to become Warriors for Change. By investing in yourself in our goods and services, know that you are funding freedom for those who need our help most. All royalties from our goods and services fund life saving services that are part of Elite's **Pathway to Their Freedom**. For more information about our community services please visit www. EliteFundsFreedom.org

The Foundation is able to expand the work that it does with survivors of human exploitation in all its ugly forms and victims of sex trafficking, due to the generosity, integrity and commitment from all our trustees, board members, community partners, donors, volunteers and you, the socially conscious consumer.

Each of our collaborative books in our world class international bestselling series features dozens of writers, who like you had a dream to become an author, and an impactful message to share with the world. We would like to thank each contributing author for their authenticity, transparency and contribution to the literary work in Chosen. Each author is a **Thriving-Survivor and Warrior for Change**.

Our production services that include Indie publishing and content creation are predicated on the belief that your story matters and that storytelling is the **Key to Your Success**. If you have an interest in sharing your story, we are happy to receive a request for consideration by writing to: ElitePublisher@ EliteFundsFreedom.org subsequent to receipt of your request for a consultation, our dedicated literary staff will contact you, provide a NDA and walk you through the next steps to becoming an author.

We would like to extend a warm Thank You of appreciation to our production team members, who specialize in working with writers, who are at different stages of the writing process.

Whether you are interested in being a contributing author in one of our collaborative world class international bestselling book series, or you have a book idea, or a developed concept, we have the tailored service that will meet your needs.

On behalf of Elite Foundation's Board of Trustees, Wendy Elliott, and myself, Dr. Jessica Vera, thank you for purchasing our goods and services.

Know that it takes just $4.11 a day, to set a survivor on the **Pathway to Their Freedom.**

Onward and upward Warriors!

#END HUMAN EXPLOITATION

#ENDHUMANTRAFFICKING

#IT ENDS WITH US

Made in the USA
Columbia, SC
12 October 2021